69.95

© Copyright 2000
J.P. van der Walt and Son (Pty.) Ltd.
380 Bosman Street, Pretoria
Set in 11 on 12.6 pt Palatino
Set by Setmate HC CC
Printed by CLF-Drukkery, 39 Blignaut Street, Bloemfontein
Cover photo: Paul A. Coetzer *The road down Elands' Pass*
Cover design: Mandi Printers CC, Murrayfield, Pretoria

First imprint 2000

ISBN 0 7993 2772 7

For Christiaan

The Hell

valley of the lions

Gamkaskloof
The most isolated valley in South Africa

Sue van Waart

J P van der Walt
Pretoria

Contents

The Hell

A land surveyor's description, dated 1841, of Gamkaskloof reads as follows: "It is bounded on the East, West, South and North by mountains."

Ask anyone in South Africa where Gamkaskloof is and the majority will not know. Ask where "Die Hel" (The Hell) is and many will know, even though they have not been there.

In a small graveyard lies the remains of J J Marais who was born in 1919 and who died in 1962. Though his bones may rot in Hell, it is a select few who find their last resting place in such idyllic surroundings, which offer serenity to the most disturbed soul (the foreign tourist).

Margaret Stoddard and her party "negotiated *Die Leer* (the ladder) *voetjie-vir-voetjie* (inch by inch) on that terrible route, for one misstep, and you would fall into forever! *Sommerso* (just like that), with your eyes open, you *voeter* (tumble) into Hell."

When he and his bulldozer made the road down into Gamkaskloof, Koos van Zyl often escaped a *gat-oor-kop* (head over heels) entry into The Hell.

The road to Hell was made with good intentions.

When there's an oncoming car, you pray that God be with you.

6

At the foot of Die Leer is a stream surrounded by trees and soft, emerald-green grass. When you lie down to rest your exhausted, aching body, the biblical Psalm 23 comes to mind.

Thought Hell does not freeze over? It did. And it does.

Introduction

When you first see the portals of The Hell from the winding road criss-crossing the Swartberg summit it's a sight you never want to forget. You know instantly how inappropriate the name *The Hell* is. And together with the Kloof folk you dissociate yourself from this unsuitable nickname.

Yet you realise it has come to stay.

The people of the valley refer to themselves as Kloovers (pronounced Cloovirs).

Stop in the right spot and you see two mighty precipices, two rocky krantzes forming a "V" with a flat floor. The mountainside is covered in green — even in winter — behind a transparent gossamer curtain of the palest blue haze. It is the most beautiful sight imaginable.

Many words have been spoken and written about this natural cultural historical valley: sense and nonsense, and fact and fabrication by both those in the know and ignoramuses.

Gamkaskloof, according to an academic, "is a subculture of South Africa because of the interaction with the surroundings which is affected by space and time."

Like the forest workers of Harkerville near Plettenberg Bay and Knysna, like the peoples of Bushmanland on the South African West Coast and like the small fishing communities strung like pearls along the Cape coast, the Gamkaskloovers lived in isolation for more than a century.

Gamkaskloof was seldom exposed to external influences. It is a sub-system to be judged against a wider ecological background.

Although there is an abundance of rivers and rivulets, water for domestic use comes from the many fountains springing from the mountain peaks.

The midsummer heat is mitigated by a gentle breeze which seems omnipresent. This keeps the Kloof cooler than nearby Oudtshoorn, Calitzdorp and Prince Albert.

The towering mountain peaks keep fierce winds as well as the massive cloud formations which bring rainstorms at bay.

As a matter of fact, this unique valley has a unique micro-climate.

The vegetation is diverse and 4 500 plant species were recorded by the year 2000. There are at least four rare animal, three rare fish and four rare rodent species.

This is where the black, the fish and the martial eagles nest.

All these findings did not bother the Kloovers unduly. Their beautiful surroundings had been part of everyday life. They saw the gentle gold beams of the sun at dawn, and the shades of mauve which painted the valleys and gorges at sunset.

Every sunny day they lived behind the rainbow of colours which filtered through the fleecy mist, so much a part of Gamkaskloof.

Early morning they saw the "copper star" rising.

This huge kloof in the Swartberg Mountains has, at different stages, been described as a breath-taking natural phenomenon.

It is a glimpse at contrasts. There is the drier, lonelier south called Onderplaas (lower farm) and the greener softer northern side called Boplaas (upper farm).

There are two distinct phases in the community — before the road and after the road — each with its peculiar characteristics.

The road was opened in 1963 and in 1992 the last inhabitant left the Kloof. Both these phases will be dealt with in this book. So too will life in the valley and a few of its colourful people — the last of their line — be discussed. Their way of living and doing is what these stories are mostly about. There are facts. And as many fabrications; some quite truthful. Facts will remain facts, but every Kloover admits frankly that *voortyd* (literally pre-times) stories are as richly spiced as the *braairibbetjie* (barbecued rib) they love.

And surely no lover of folklore dare ignore a good story even if the foundations are a bit shaky.

Because the Kloof can only be reached via the Swartberg Pass — one of the most formidable passes in the country, some say in the world, with the exception of the Darjeeling Pass in Tibet —you will linger on this road which leads to Gamkaskloof. It is part of a total "Kloof experience".

You are going to meet some of the earliest dwellers, the Khoi (called Hottentots by the Kloovers) and the San or Bushmen. And learn the tales of pioneer whites who came seemingly from nowhere and tamed the mystic valley.

There was and is no "canned" entertainment. The Kloof did not have electricity until the mid 1990s and even at the turn of the twentieth century it is limited to one or two houses. Light at night came from candles and paraffin lamps. That is why most evenings were spent round huge fires, in or out of doors, and the art of conversation — story-telling and singing, and games like riddles — was practised. Perhaps that is the reason why so many of the stories of *voortye* are well remembered.

The stories are as varied as life itself. They are about love and heartache, happiness and sorrow, pain and suffering, and life and death. They are also about those who are supposed to "rest in peace" but will not or cannot.

Above all, these stories want to tell about generations of people who survived nature's hardships, being tougher than most of their contemporaries; pioneers who did not shirk a life that offered few creature comforts. They survived, remained civilised and raised healthy children. These people were pounded, kneaded and shaped by the elements of nature. Those who know no better might describe their lifestyle as "wild" or "uncultured". People with a sense of values know that they were well-adapted "children" of their natural habitat.

To live in isolation maintaining high and healthy moral values with a childlike faith in their Maker and raise morally strong families, is a huge responsibility.

The Kloovers were a group of Afrikaners who maintained their human dignity, their identity, spoke colourful Afrikaans, made a good living and retained a sense of humour.

This book is not an attempt to record the history of Gamkaskloof. It is the STORY in the HISTORY. It is a peephole into the life of people of yore and the stories of a group of people who lived in a unique world of their own making.

There are few tourist attractions as well known to the outside world. People who go there with an attitude of "Here I am! Entertain me and keep me busy!" will be disappointed.

Yet visitors love the place and their numbers are increasing rapidly. Many purely wish to get away from the asphalt jungle, crowded cities, and the stress and pressure of corporate life.

They braai their chops and *boerewors* (sausages) on the river bank and leave with an impression that "there is nothing to see".

That is not how you should visit Gamkaskloof.

The joy of a visit is to experience the BEING, the WAS and the IS. To walk in the footsteps of Kloovers; in nature. Listen to the birdsong. See and smell the flowers. Experience the tranquillity. No traffic, no crime, freedom from care and the all-encompassing solitude. Timelessness. To hear the baboons *bôgom* (the sound made by baboons) high in the krantzes. Hear the river in the pebble beds; gossip with the birds.

The Hell is a paradise for hikers and walkers who wish to visit the waterfall at Elandspad high up in the Swartberg Mountains; so totally unspoilt and natural. It falls wide and clear over a sheer precipice between two giant rocks polished to a sheen through the ages.

It sometimes happens that the Gamka (lion) and the Dwyka (lioness) rivers are in flood simultaneously. It is a spectacular sight when this natural phenomenon occurs. The two rivers meet at a bottleneck. Two distinctive colours of muddy water are clearly visible. The rivers push and battle for the right to be the first to empty their waters through the narrow gorge. One pushes the other back. Power builds up. One must win. When victory comes, a thunderous explosion reverberates in the valley like a vicious thunderstorm. Lion versus lioness in the battle for supremacy.

This is one explanation for the name *Skietkrans*.

Kloovers say that the huge rocks in the river-bed were thrown there by lightning during thunderstorms. The fury of such storms is an awesome sight.

Lightning flashes play with gigantic boulders like children playing *klip-klippie* (throwing stones). Many is the time that overawed Kloovers peeped through the curtains after a particularly loud crash to watch the results of the elements' frolicking.

Teenek (Tea Neck) is next to the waterfall. Then follows Snaar (string) where an enormous boulder lies across the river. This rock, they will tell you, was thrown there by a single flash of lightning. The Kaffirskloovers remember the night it was torn from the mountain and came thundering down.

Not so many decades before the turn of the twenty-first century, a biblical-type miracle occurred in the Kloof right before the eyes of two goat herdsmen.

They were combing the mountainside for stray goats. All around was the blue of the sky with the sun shining brightly. It was a beautiful day. Their's might easily have been the first human feet to walk in that section of the Kloof.

Then it happened.

The men heard a far-off rumbling like thunder. It came closer. The earth trembled beneath their feet and then right in front of them there was the sound of a whiplash and the solid mountainside crackled. Yellowish smoke billowed out, followed by crystal-clear water.

Both men dropped to their knees with their eyes fixed on the miracle and prayed.

Forgotten were the stray goats. Awestruck, they walked back to their homes realising that they had witnessed something of the wonder of creation which they had read about in the Old Testament of the Bible. That this happened at a time when earthquakes laid the towns of Ceres, Tulbagh and Wolseley to waste, they did not know. Or that the San Andreas fault runs through the Swartberg

Mountains which makes them susceptible to earthquakes.

For the energetic hiker there is a lovely surprise. Further down from the waterfall at Osberg is a small inland lake. The road to Grootkloof leads to the waterfall. Keep on walking and you come to a place where you gaze up to the blue sky which seems no bigger than the circle of two hands. That is where the witkruis eagle keeps. Tree ferns and kiepersol (umbrella trees) abound with stately arum lilies growing from the rocks.

The pool below the waterfall is called Grootkloofmeer (Great Kloof Lake). On a warm summer's day this place is heaven on earth. The sound of falling water drowns out all other sounds.

Look around and you see caves. There are many caves in the Kloof as well as Bushman paintings (as rock art is colloquially known).

Not far from the house of Willem and Lenie Marais is Drosterskloof (Deserters' Kloof). Close by is a rectangular cave with several well-preserved paintings.

Gamkaskloof's newspaper can be read daily in the winding dust road which runs through the valley.

Every *spoor* (track) tells a story. You see which *spoor* leads from where to where. You "read" that the giant kudu bull was in this or that garden. You wonder why the other five were not there. The baboons were up to mischief in the Esterhuizen's graveyard where the headstones were left upended in the baboons' quest for their favourite snack of scorpions. Their manure, like so many black, twisted soft ice creams, are all over the place.

The porcupines are becoming increasingly cheeky, making holes right in the middle of the road.

You walk on and look at the homes of former dwellers. And the style of the houses. And the furniture. And you wonder how these things got there. Perhaps you have already heard that everything in the valley — before the road — was carried in on human shoulders: piece by single piece.

Tonight you sit round a huge bonfire — in winter.

Summer nights you sit on the open *stoep* (veranda) and watch the sun go down.

You help light the candles and the paraffin lamps.

When the full moon comes out over the valley, it is movingly beautiful. The whole valley is bathed in a clear, gentle, almost unearthly light. You get up and walk for miles in this magical atmosphere.

You have been warned to go softly past the Esterhuizen graves. Something strange might happen. If you feel an icy chill moving from your feet up to your head, and your scalp starts tingling, you have "experienced" The Hell's graveyard.

Back home, even on the coldest winter night, you are warm from your walk and ready for a bath. And bed. And when you feel the icy cold of The Hell, you are thankful that you do not have to sleep in the open in a sleeping bag when frost turns to ice early in the evening.

In your bedroom you feel at home. You are surrounded by caring people — people who want you there, people who also care about the Kloof and its uniqueness and wish to keep it unspoilt for generations to come. Gamkaskloof is a place for lingering, walking, hiking, climbing and inspecting … and for enjoying the food as it was prepared on the open fires by the *voormense* (early inhabitants).

You long too taste the Hanepoot raisins — sweeter than any other raisins — and the dried figs — more delicious than any other dried figs.

Perhaps the soil has something to do with it. Or

15

maybe it is because your senses have become un-cluttered.

Even after the first day in the Kloof, outside things fade and do not seem so very important any more: not newspapers nor the city. Cement and asphalt are very, very far away. In the Kloof you are in a world where all you desire is to live in harmony with nature.

In these things and in the stories of the *voormense* lie the pleasure of a visit to The Hell.

The Hell?

Gamkaskloof!

It's a heavenly experience!

Author's note

I t was impossible to convey the atmosphere created by such a totally Afrikaans community in a formal English translation. It was like taking a Kloover out of his valley and displaying him to a "circus crowd".

I decided to bring the "outsider" into Die Kloof and introduce him or her to the people against their own background. For these folk, who speak a colourful and very descriptive Afrikaans, "ordinary English" seemed out of character. I tried to keep to their own vernacular and write Afrikaans in English.

I hope the experiment succeeded.

The Author

Chapter one
Cave dwellers

Like the rest of South Africa, The Hell was known to indigenous peoples before it was given this nickname. Only the San, named *Bushmen* by early settlers, left a record of their stay. Unfortunately, only their rock art remnants are left with no record of times or dates.

Like the two periods in Gamkaskloof, the before and after-the-road eras, there are two earlier before and after eras: before and after the whites.

Thunberg, an early traveller, documented the times when the settlers arrived. The Bushmen were seemingly intent on annihilating the whites, and stealing their livestock was general practice.

Thunberg describes a commando who had shot and killed a hundred Bushmen and another division who had eradicated 400. The government supplied arms and ammunition. Although the commandos suffered casualties, there were no deaths.

A medical doctor in the company relates how he used a mixture of gunpowder and urine as antidote to the poisoned arrows of the Bushmen.

All agreed that the Bushmen knew no fear of death.

So numerous were the Bushmen at the end of the eighteenth century and so strong their resistance to "opponents", that they had almost eradicated the Khoi or Hottentots as they were known. They very nearly succeeded in doing the same with the white settlers.

By the 1770s white pioneers had reached the Sneeu-berge (Snow Mountains) north of Graaff-Reinet. There were so many Bushmen in the area that it was called *Boesmanstreek* (Bushmen region).

Huge commandos combining Khoi and settlers fought their common enemy, the Bushmen. In one skirmish they cornered 500 or more Bushmen. In spite of the fact that the Bushmen attacked any *trekker* (migrant) and had stolen 11 000 sheep, they relented and did not harm them.

After this incident, the government — represented by governor Macartney — changed official policy and decreed that Bushmen could only be shot if the life of the farmer or that of his family was threatened. They had to be left with their rights intact, in their traditional dwelling places, not be molested nor could their children be abducted as slaves.

The farmers adhered to this law and went further by hunting zebra and handing this, their favourite meat, to the Bushmen.

Missionaries tried to start a school for them.

The Dutch East India Company who followed the British rule, however, continued to eradicate Bushmen between 1786 and 1797, when an estimated 2 500 were shot and killed and 600 captured.

Another early traveller, Lichtenstein, medic and botanist toured the Cape.

He recorded a different view of the Bushmen and their rights. He believed greed for the riches of the new settlers enticed them from their traditional homes on the banks of the Great (Orange) River. The Cape province was not their original territory.

"They only brought their most injurious warfare and were not there to fight for their birthrights," he states.

Whatever the reasons, the colonists were in constant danger during the Bushmen "reign". No farmer dared move more than a few hundred feet from his house without a gun. Farmers were killed and often whole families murdered. Abandoned farms with ripe crops on the land were not an unusual sight.

The Bushmen were cunning. In several cases they hired themselves out to gullible farmers to mind the livestock. Such a man was a gem. He knew the best grazing and had a knack for handling animals. However, as soon as he knew the lie of the land, he would inform his fellow Bushmen and when the farmer came to his senses, he was without livestock and herdsman.

For almost a century the battle between colonists and Bushmen continued. The last three decades of the eighteenth century were decisive and many Bushmen retreated to the Kalahari desert.

A family story told in The Hell pictures the times.

The paterfamilias had gangrene and for years he agonised, yet could not give up the ghost. It was so bad that his wife had to use pure alcohol to clean her hands before and after attending to him.

The old folks wondered out loud what kept the man earthbound and suffering so intensely.

One day his young granddaughter, having heard the adults talk, asked him straight out and to the point: "*Oupa* (Grandfather), why can't you die?"

He told her a gruesome tale.

In the early years when Bushmen were hunted he was sent on a mission by the authority in Graaff-Reinet to eradicate Bushmen in the Swartberg Mountains. He followed a trail into Gamkaskloof where he cornered a family in a cave and killed them. He saved the life of a tiny girl, to take home for his wife to tame as a housemaid.

The girl sat in front of him on his horse.

As soon as they started to move, she viciously bit him on the forearm. He was so shocked and furious that he flung her from the horse. Her head hit a stone and she died.

These were the reasons why he was suffering so badly.

Soon after the confession, the grandfather died.

His son took over the farm.

One day he was in the mountains looking for goats, when he came upon the caves. He recognised them from his daughter's description. They did not look abandoned but gave the impression that the inhabitants had gone away for a short while.

The clay pots were there. Even the ashes lay undisturbed. And, in addition, there were many Bushmen paintings. One of them made him think that they had monitored the commandos' comings and goings for some time. The evidence: a painting of a farmer on horseback, a hat on his head, gun slung across his shoulders and a dog trotting alongside. He wanted to take one of the clay pots home but thought better of it. He did, however, put a small bag made of animal skin in his pocket. When he took it out at home, he found it had turned into powder.

The story was told to the next generation.

One day a granddaughter decided to visit the caves. Her son and a young man Hans Kleurling, wanted to go along. They followed a route past one of the fountains. Halfway up the mountain they came to a fork in the path and took the one where a huge old aloe grew as the early tales indicated.

They climbed higher and higher, but the caves were still distant and the day was running out.

The granddaughter split from the other two and tried a shorter, more direct route when she stumbled and fell into what she describes as "a huge marble-like bath". It was so slippery she could not get out.

"Is this Bushmen revenge?" she wondered as she shouted, prayed, shouted and prayed.

After what seemed like forever, Hans Kleurling arrived to look for her. He could not help her. He walked round and round but try as he might, not even their fingertips touched.

"Miss, you'll have to pray."

"Dear God, man! I have prayed using every word in the dictionary!" she snapped.

Then Hans prayed. A moving prayer.

He walked round the stone basin which held her captive, and lo and behold at a point their fingers touched. Very cautiously she stretched and he stretched. Eventually he got her out.

They returned home. But since then another generation has vowed to visit the caves and spend the night there.

Bushmen cruelties and Khoi tortures are part of the folk-tales told by earlier generations.

Avantine, a Bushman captain, was particularly cruel. Khoi were mercilessly tortured. They were scalped, their nails plucked out and while still alive, they were disembowelled.

It was a dirty war.

Korêl was a one-eyed Bushman famous for his keen shooting and for being notoriously cruel.

Uithaalder was another.

The Khoi were not taking this lying down. They replied in kind.

Magistrate Andries Stockenström described a scene in which Bushmen were left to die most horribly.

During a skirmish, the Khoi captured a community of Bushmen. Babes in arms were thrown on a heap, straw strewn over them and they were set alight. Older children were immobilised by cutting chunks of flesh from the soles of their feet and were left to die of thirst and hunger, after the nails of their fingers had been plucked off.

Old Kloof families had a wealth of Bushmanlore.

One of the tales concerned a Steenkamp family whose father fought to the death but managed to save his wife and 14 children.

Bushmen sent threats to frighten farmers off their land. If they stayed, they were attacked.

Carel Cordier's *Voormense* often found their tobacco lands stripped after a night raid by the Bushmen. They were shot when caught; evidence that the Bushmen were around after Kloovers had settled in.

Sir John Barrow, a British traveller in days gone by, has little sympathy for the whites but admits that they lived in constant danger.

Who are these people who came to live in the Swartberg and Gamkaskloof caves?

They were the first human creatures to inhabit the subcontinent and a large section of East Africa before black or white people did so.

They are the last remnants of Africa's hunting peoples.

Dr Brian du Toit of Florida University made a study of "modern" Gamkaskloovers and found them to be of the most isolated people in the world. If they were to disappear, they would have even more in common with their predecessors.

There are similarities in naming traditions. Like old Afrikaner families, Bushmen gave a newborn a grandparent's name. They believed that people with similar names were related. A girl with the same name as one from another tribe would be called her "cousin". They would visit each other even if they lived far apart. Bushmen of different tribes had different dressing habits. Their art styles are different. The best-known relics of Bushman culture are found in considerable numbers in the Swartberg Mountains and in Gamkaskloof. The Kloof Bushmen were most likely !Xam (the ! is a Bushman click sound), an extinct tribe.

They were the ones who painted on cave walls and mountain overhangs. The Kalahari Bushmen, for instance, were not rock artists.

Their paintings mostly depict hunting scenes, medicine-makers dancing, the healing of people and the changing of man into animal which they believed happened to humans in extreme dancing ecstacy.

Where the white Kloover in his isolation depended on prayer and herbal medicines gathered in the veld, the Bushmen healed themselves through spiritual discipline in dance.

Quite a bit is known about their spiritual values.

The mythical *hotnotsgot* (praying mantis) in various shapes is a god honoured by all Bushmen. It had the power to resurrect a whole ostrich from a water pool when only a bloodstained feather was thrown in.

The god can transform into human shape and return as one of a bygone generation.

He finds his grandson with an eye ripped out by a baboon who plays a ballgame with it. The praying mantis joins him, catches the eye, throws it in the pool and the child is resurrected.

A German scientist, Wilhelm Bleek, studied the Bushmen in the late nineteenth century and recorded numerous stories about !Kaggen, a god who took the shape of a stock insect (praying mantis). !Kaggen could create other living beings and equip them with unique characteristics.

He could make animals do things against their will. Bushmen prayed to the moon. The moon brought rain. Rain was respected because it was often accompanied by thunder and lightning which struck sinners. Girls in particular were vulnerable. That was one of the reasons why women seldom walked in the rain. Girls who were struck and killed by lightning became stars in the sky. Clouds were the hair of people who had died.

The Bushmen's involvement in, and preoccupation with, rain and water are understandable, particularly after they had gone to live in desert territory. In later years the name *Bushman* was exchanged for *San*; a Khoi name meaning "collector".

Some students maintain that concepts of tribe, race and nation were non-existent in the San culture. There were Bushmen and there were animals. That was all.

Another thing which Kloovers of all colours always had in common was their love of honey. Wherever he went, the Bushman was on the lookout for bees. Stones were arranged as beacons of "property rights". Such a nest became "the holy property of the finder" and heaven help the one who removed the honey from a marked nest!

Cases are known where honey thieves were killed.

The Reverend John Campbell of the London Mission Society noted in 1813 that all Bushmen claimed all rights to mountain honey as their rightful property.

As a farmer marked his cattle and his sheep, so the Bushman marked his honey. When a white farmer, ignorant of this practice, removed the honey, the Bushman would take a cow or a ewe from his herd.

Whites soon became wise to this and traded with the Bushmen.

Decades after the Bushmen had disappeared from the Kloof, remnants of their stone beacons, rope ladders and wooden pegs in rock crevices serve as evidence of their days of honey hunting.

It was not unusual to see a Bushman digging for plants and roots, and carrying them home in his hunting bag.

Collecting veld fruit, however, was the task of women.

Women were the providers of food for the family. Edible plants were collected and if everyone was not completely satisfied after a meal, the woman was regarded as being lazy and her family complained vociferously.

Plant-gathering expeditions were happy occasions. The children went along and learnt from their mothers what was used for what purpose.

A hard, sharpened stick was used to dig. Water in an ostrich egg shell was carried in a net made of sinews.

Women never went to the veld on their own. They believed a baboon lay in wait for lonely women.

Men hunted in groups because a buck was too heavy for one to carry.

The Bushman, whose sense of smell was not as keen as an animal's, relied on his sensitive, well-developed perceptive faculties to find a *spoor* (footprint). News was written in the sand, as the modern Kloovers also learnt. Add to this that he hunted with a short hand weapon and he had to be an expert in animal behaviour. He moved quietly in order not to alarm or warn the prey.

Generally, the largest animal was chosen. It provided the most food. Meat was shared so that it could not go bad.

Two other traditions were shared by all Kloovers: the making of bonfires and fireside story-telling.

Fires were made outside every "house". It was the heart and soul of Bushman family life. Bushmen lived round the fire, cooked on it and talked. At night they often slept round the fire — women separately.

In the morning the fire was covered with ashes in such a way as to keep a pilot flame going.

At the fireside, folklore was repeated and often recreated. As in old Afrikaner folktales many stories were about jackal. These animals were the clever, cunning ones. In many Bushmen tales the jackal symbolised the white farmer.

The Bushmen played games; even ball games. One of the games played by the Nharo tribe was called *!wi'um* — one, two — in it counting was necessary. They drew games in the sand; complicated ones in which 64 tiny holes were made in four rows and small stones were used as counters.

Bushmen loved music and dancing. Singing accompanied their dancing. A small mouth harp with a bow at one end and a string in the mouth pulled by the finger was a favourite instrument.

Thumb pianos comprised a wooden block with prongs plucked by the thumb. Each prong had a different tone.

Instruments were for recreation. Dancing and music were religious and ritualistic.

Visitations by spirits were regular occurrences at dances. Although spirits were regarded as evil, they helped to relieve tension and animosity, and healed the sick.

Throughout the centuries, Bushmen exercised birth control. Survival required that these nomads have no more than three, maximum four children. Ideal spacing was four years apart.

The size of a family determined the survival of the whole tribe. That was why pregnant women went to the bush to give birth. They returned alone. More often than not, the newborn was left for the hyenas.

Missionaries who tried to "civilise" these people had little, if any, understanding of their habits. They were judged by Western standards. They expected these children of nature to do "an honest day's work in the fields". This went completely against their grain, as they were essentially hunters.

Polygamy was denounced even when there was a general scarcity of males. Bushmen did not possess many earthly belongings — only what they could carry.

They adored giving presents. When two people had had an argument, a gift had to be exchanged "because it softens the heart". To refuse such an offering was malicious.

Gifts consisted of ostrich eggshells, eland fat, beads, skins and knives, among other things. Rifts were healed out and not left to smoulder.

Bushmanlore tells of N!aba who was cross with her husband Dam because he never gathered firewood and sat chatting with friends all day long. He was quick-tempered so she could not talk to him. She then started telling everyone how difficult it was to live with such a man. Initially, no-one listened to her and Dam just carried on.

N!aba did not give up and eventually everyone could see the truth of her complaints. They agreed with her.

That was when Dam realised that no-one approved of his behaviour, and reformed and became a better husband.

Bushmen were usually an uncomplicated people. If there was a dispute, it was recognised, aired and good relations restored.

When the community showed their disapproval of something, the sinner heard about it from them.

Whereas social fires were revived at night, it was totally different during rituals. Fires had to be made afresh, with the traditional spark from the rubbing together of sticks.

Rituals were the Bushman's link to the temporal world, the power of creation, death and transition.

Information gathered by modern researchers indicates that Bushmen believed in two gods, a major and a minor one. One god was good and "heavenly" by nature and the other evil or "hellish".

The Reverend Campbell of the London Mission Society tried to teach the Bushmen Western values.

He could hardly believe it when a Bushman whom he thought to have a good grasp of the difference between "good" and "bad" formulated: "It is bad when another Bushman sleeps with your wife, but it is good when you sleep with his wife."

At the turn of the twentieth century, there was an estimated 55 000 Bushmen left. However, there were none in Gamkaskloof. They were scattered in Namibia, Angola and Zambia with fewer than a hundred in South Africa.

Bushmen who refused to be employed by whites became squatters somewhere or grouped in gangs who existed by stealing meat in order to feed their families.

Their traditional social order disappeared. Women relied on their husband's wages for existence and survival. Some actually became prostitutes.

Yet in spite of their almost pathetic circumstances, the Bushmen who were interviewed did not long for their earlier "natural" existence. They wanted riches and status.

White standards. Western standards.

An ancient Bushmen tale became a reality.

"One day the god arranged a tug-o'-war. One end of the rope was given to a Bushman and the other to a Tswana. They pulled and pulled. The rope broke. The Tswana's end was made of leather. The Bushman's of grass."

Was this symbolic of the economy?

Age-old practices and traditions no longer exist. Nothing took their place.

Between the last white Kloovers and the earliest Bushman Kloovers there is a generation gap of easily 10 000 years. Calculated in time, it is not so long ago that the only footsteps in the Kloof were bare ones made by the small hunters whom the first whites called *'Bosjesmans'*.

The places where the earliest civilisations met were at fountains and watering places where man and animal quenched their thirst. When exactly shoe treads came to the Kloof is open to speculation. Cases are known where Bushmen joined farmers and became excellent herdsmen.

The whites eventually succeeded in driving the Bushmen from Gamkaskloof, but they had no success with the other, almost human, co-inhabitants, namely the baboons.

Dwellers in The Hell since time immemorial, the baboons were, and are, the most difficult creatures to get rid of and they survive the longest.

Perhaps because they did not try to capture everything for themselves or tried to eliminate the people but coexisted with them, albeit on their own terms.

Their *spoor* (footprints) is everywhere in Gamkaskloof; in the sand and in their daily existence.

The commonest kind is the chacma, a dog-faced brown animal.

Since earliest times, the baboon has seldom been accepted by man as a friend, but regarded as a pest.

Very few stories of tame baboons exist in the Swartberg Mountains. In Gamkaskloof there are none.

Dowe (deaf) Hendrik Schoeman of Schoemanshoek at the foot of the Swartberg lives on in mountainlore because many moons ago he had a tame baboon who travelled with his transport wagon trains. This baboon would amuse everyone during the long, tedious journeys. Sometimes he would grab someone's hat, put it on his own head and comically sit on the neck of an ox.

His most amusing trick was to run treadmill style on the wheel of an ox-wagon.

Baboons are immensely destructive. Even the hated jackal catches and kills for food only, but not so the baboon — he is more cruel than the Bushmen.

Baboons will catch a young animal, dig out its eyes, eat them and then tear out the *melkpensie* (abomasum) for the milk and leave the lamb to die.

A whole field of mealies, watermelon, *spanspek* (melon), pumpkins, you name it, is often plundered for a bite from each.

When whites came to the Kloof, baboons were a huge problem. They generally kept to the high reaches of the mountains and no krantz was too steep for them to clamber up out of gun reach. Baboons are wily, and to trap one is difficult. Now and again one was caught in a trap and shot.

Their bereavement was almost human. For days, sometimes weeks, they would stay away but once memories had faded, they would be back.

One of the baboons, called Bloubek (blue mouth), was "a devil" who feared no man nor beast.

Maybe he was a deposed leader. He was so fearless that not even a farmer — and the baboons feared males — frightened him. His appetite ran to the best mealies of the crop. He would pick one, take a bite, throw it away and try another.

After he had had an entrée of pumpkin or watermelon, a huge ripe fruit would be ruined by one bite.

Fig trees next to a homestead were not left unscathed. Even the reed platforms on which fruit was dried were vandalised. He did not eat much. He plundered.

The best shottists in the Kloof — and they were all excellent — could not get rid of him.

If baboons were unloved and useless, the *dassies* (rock rabbits, hyrax) were different. They seemed to have been there forever. The beautiful little furry creatures with their gentle eyes are still as abundant as in the early days. They were useful. Skins were used by early dwellers for many purposes. Troglodytes who dwelled in the Swartberg caves maintained their meat was the tastiest of all wildlife and even better than the tenderest lamb.

The *dassie's* urine was, and is, sought after for medical purposes. *Dassies* have natural "toilets" in caves and always return to the same place.

Thunberg, an early scientist and traveller, recorded a tar-like mound colonists called *dassiepis* (dassie urine). The little creature apparently does not drink much fluids with the result that its urine is thick and "gluey". This was used as medicine.

Nowadays, it has the scientific name of hyracium.

Voormense used it to treat hysterics, epilepsy, St Vitus's dance, and many other ailments.

A *sieketrooster* (curate) the Reverend H King thought very highly of its medicinal qualities. It was used against "hypocondria, hysterical nerves and similar conditions which doctors could not explain," he explained.

Dr A Brown believes the value of the urine lies in the herbal diet of the animal. It contains buchu in highly concentrated doses.

Dr Brown recorded that the Khoi boiled it and the end-result was applied in the treatment of poisoning, back aches and stomach pains.

It was dried, powdered and rubbed into wounds after snake bites or scorpion stings.

In modern times the *dassiepis* is used in refined medicines, mostly for kidney disorders.

Part of the Kloovers' survival was their excellent shooting. (During the Anglo-Boer War — 1899 to 1902 — they even experimented with heavier weapons. A hollow tree trunk was loaded with gunpowder and stones ready for a British attack.)

Kloovers hunted mainly for food. But vermin brought money.

The government, represented by the magistrates of Calitzdorp and Prince Albert, paid £5 for a leopard skin and £2.10s for a jackal tail. Even a baboon tail was worth something.

There were many vermin to contend with: wild cats, otters, beavers and polecats to name but a few. Many caught the farmers' chickens and robbed the nests of eggs. But the most feared was the *tier* (leopard). Man and animal had a healthy respect for this animal which bordered on fear.

The Elands Pass road leading downward. (Photograph: Paul A. Coetzer)

The view of the ravine from the west side. (Photograph: Paul A. Coetzer)

i

Zannie and Anita van der Walt of Nature Conservation on the stoep of Piet Swanepoel's house who was the last resident in the valley. The Van der Walts have lived in and worked from the house since 1991. (Photograph: Paul A. Coetzer)

The house of Karel Cordier and Andreas Marais in Kafferskloof. The two families shared the house. It contains two kitchens and two bathrooms. (Photographs: Paul A. Coetzer)

Chapter two

Gamkaskloof — valley of the lions

Leopards, called *tiers* by the Kloovers, are still to be found in the Swartberg Mountains.

Lions, like the original Kloovers, are no more. Not even in mountain lore. They live on only in name. Yet they must have been there. The name *Gamkaskloof* indicates that they must have been numerous even if not predominant.

Who or what caused them to become extinct is not recorded.

For many centuries the Swartberg Mountains kept the people in its basin, and away from the outside world. The chain of mountains which surround the Little Karoo is formidable and the most spectacular mountain chain in the country. The range forms a 200 km barricade between the Great and Little Karoo.

This basin was formerly called *Cango* by the Khoi. Some say it means 'water from the mountains'. Others say it means 'clean, clear water'.

At 2 326 m or 7 600 ft, the Seweweeks (Seven Week) Mountain is the tallest in the chain.

The Swartberg Mountains' original stone deposits are twisted and tortured into the most fantastic shapes and magnificent colours, ranging from browns and reds to pinks and yellows. For many centuries the native mountain folk, hunters, children of nature, must have known that the Swartberg Mountain hid a secret valley — the fertile Gamkaskloof.

Swartberg Pass held the key to the modern access to the Kloof and to its discovery by outsiders in the nineteenth and twentieth centuries; a hiding place of exceptional communities.

Before reaching Gamkaskloof, the motorist must negotiate the Swartberg Pass.

This pass, which was completed by Thomas Bain (son of Andrew Geddes who built the Bainskloof Pass near Cape Town), is one of the most spectacular in the country, not only for its scenic vistas but also for its wild flowers, buck and unspoilt natural surroundings.

The pass crosses the Swartberg between Oudtshoorn and Prince Albert, and is a tame indication of what is waiting on the winding, twisting dirt road of Gamkaskloof near the entry into the Valley.

Swartberg Pass remains a monument to the skill of Thomas Bain.

This author still believes that Bain learnt the unique "dry method" of laying stone walls from the earliest white Cango settlers.

On my small farm in Schoemanspoort at the foot of the pass there used to be remnants of the very first road the farmers built (1752 onward) when they settled there. They shaped and stacked stone wedges, and filled and solidified the structure, not with clay or cement but with small stones.

I acquired the land in order to preserve this last few hundred-metre stretch of pioneering history. When the Oudtshoorn Municipality laid water pipes in 1992, and while in the process of acquiring servitudes, they blasted the road. Not a piece of the road was left.

This method used for retaining walls was the same as that which Bain had used so successfully. In fact, the Swartberg Pass is intact even after having been rocked by several severe earthquakes.

Negotiating and enjoying this beautiful pass should be part of the traveller's trip to The Hell.

The road through Meiringspoort was the first to connect the Little Karoo with the hinterland. But it was still a long route for the Cango farmers who wanted the tracks that they used, to be replaced with a road across the mountain close to Prince Albert.

In 1881, Mr Tassie, with the help of a hundred Mozambicans, was contracted to build a route across the Swartberg and was allocated £18 000 for that purpose.

He soon went bankrupt and a Member of Parliament, Sir Henry Juta, obtained permission and the services of Thomas Bain to complete the pass. (The book *Swartberg en Sy Mense* tells the complete story.)

Today, this pass is a silent witness to the penalty paid by hundreds of convicts who were sentenced to many years of *hardepad* (literally hard road = hard labour) for a variety of crimes.

At the lower end of the scale was the *kettingspan* (chain team). They were chained together and worked near the camping site. At the top of the scale was the *koffiespan* (coffee team), criminals who qualified for tobacco and coffee.

These convicts built huts for themselves from stones on the mountain. Remnants of the "jail houses" can be seen to this day. A house could sleep about 30 people.

One night, during a particularly heavy snow storm, the roof of a house collapsed and killed all the inmates.

In the mountains there is a graveyard where an estimated 150 of these pass builders found a final resting place. Many died of illness probably caused by exposure. Some tried to bolt, only to find a worse fate.

Thomas Bain used varying numbers of workers as the work load required and it is said that at times there were a thousand.

These people had to be fed.

Young Jim Stockenström from Prince Albert and his bride of a few months were allocated a contract to cater for them.

Rations are reputed to have been a loaf of bread a day per person, meat stew from 16 sheep and an ox, with dried beans or peas as additional protein.

The first official road user was Colonel Schermbrucker, Commissioner of Public Works in the Cape Colony. He opened the pass in January 1887.

The convict labour cost the government £50 000. Bain had tendered £20 000 for his part of the contract, but completed it for £15 000.

The Fourie family living at the foot of the Swartberg were regular pass-users.

Oupa Ockert Fourie taught his sons a piece of mountain wisdom which stood three generations in good stead. "A horse," he said, "should never cross the pass at an irregular pace. Keep an even pace. Not faster downhill or slower uphill. You'll get to your destination quicker and the horse will live longer."

Transport riders were delighted with this shorter route to their markets inland.

They soon learnt to adapt to the circumstances of a journey which took them from a warm to hot valley, to a mountain top where the snow can lie inches thick and the wind becomes icy.

Dowe Hendrik Schoeman, a Cango transport rider, loaded hollow, porous sandstones gathered in the river, onto his wagon. This he soaked in paraffin and lit. His sons and the labourers who accompanied the wagon trains picked up small stones which they heated in the hollow basin of the large stone. The large stones were wrapped in sacks and when they reached the snow line, these sacks kept their feet warm. The small stones were put in their jacket pockets and defrosted frozen hands.

On the summit of the mountain they needed a hot drink. But sticks were damp. Another soak of the large sandstone in paraffin and they quickly got a fire going to make steaming mugs of coffee. Transport riders in their heavily loaded wagons knew that as soon as they reached McClune's Toll at the summit, the sweating animals had to be outspanned and chased below the snow line. There they were tended and brought back the following morning.

Part of the mountain stories concerns a transport rider, his wife and seven children who travelled in two wagons with a load of tobacco.

Near the top of the mountain they landed in a blinding snow storm.

To save their lives, they abandoned one of the wagons and inspanned all the oxen in front of the other hoping to reach McClune's Toll station safely. Within minutes, the story goes, the wagons were covered in snow. The oxen were cut loose to make their own way below the snow level. They did not survive.

The family found refuge in one of the convict houses and used every scrap of wood to keep warm. Food was on the wagon, but it was frozen. When the wood ran out, one of the children became ill and died. A second one went berserk with stress and ran out of the hut never to be seen again.

A third child died in the hospital at Prince Albert after the family had been rescued.

Hendrik Hanekom wrote his own legend in his lifetime.

He had the contract for the *poskoets* (mail coach).

The coach's approach was announced at stopping places all along the route by loud bugle blowing.

He had a team of 12 mules which regularly pulled up to 14 000 lb (pounds) of tobacco at a time, up and down the pass.

Many nervous passengers refused to stay in the "coffin on wheels". When they came to the zig-zags, they climbed out and walked to a straighter stretch of road.

One of Hanekom's drivers was no mean spitter. He amused passengers by gathering a ball of spit in his mouth and directing it at the inquisitive lizards knocking them off their stone perches.

There is the story of Hennie Velsambreel. He was a troglodyte.

Of him it is said that "he travelled the mountain in style". A fellow troglodyte pulled him on a sled while he sat in the shade of an umbrella made of animal skins.

Stories about this legendary character abound.

Ockert Fourie of Matjiesfontein (halfway up the pass) knew him. The old man was the harness maker for mountain folk. Ockert often took skins to him and ordered saddles or a harness, whatever his father needed. He says old Hennie had a skin problem and could not tolerate the sun. That is why a close relative agreed to pull him and the heavy umbrella around in the "home"-made sled.

The two were regulars in Prince Albert where firewood and goods such as this were exchanged for sugar, coffee and salt, among other things.

Another legend has it that Hennie's "puller" lived in a cave near him in comparative comfort. Hennie was said to have gathered a fortune in diamonds which he kept hidden in the cave.

He tended a small vegetable patch and was no

mean stone thrower. He hunted rabbits and small buck in this manner.

Another very sad but true story concerns a family whose only son was mentally unstable. When he reached puberty, the mountain folk were worried about the safety of their daughters. They also noticed that at certain times, mostly during full moon, he became violent. No-one wanted to institutionalise such a normally loving youngster.

His parents, knowing of their son's love of the freedom of the mountains, built a shelter where he could be incarcerated when necessary. Otherwise he roamed his beloved mountains.

On nights when the moon was full and the jackal howled, the sound blended with the wailing and heart-rending cries of a young man who could not understand the why's of life.

Ou Nefie (literally old cousin) was another Swartberg legend. According to mountain tales, he was "a yellow man with long, straight black hair". His mother, he told everyone who asked, was a slave with the Schoeman family of the Cango who stayed on after she had been freed in the early nineteenth century.

Ou Nefie was reputedly the richest of all the farmers in the mountain. He kept a chest full of gold pounds under his *katel* (double bed). He was granted or bought a farm from the Independent Church and planted lucrative tobacco crops. Soon this was too small for his ambitions. He offered to utilise unused farms for half the crop. People say, "he sold loads and loads of tobacco in Oudsthoorn."

Ou Nefie was thrifty to the point of being miserly. His wife knew that the heavy brown loaves she baked had to be doughy in the centre. "They are not so readily digested and you stay satisfied longer and do not eat so often and so much," he believed.

He was no mean "seamster". He wore only one pair of multicoloured pants. When he took his livestock to graze in the mountain, needle and cotton and *laslappies* (pieces of cloth) went along. There he sat naked and mended his clothes with large, strong stitches.

One of his sayings was: "No man is ever too poor to save something." He made his own shoes and seldom spent money.

When a farmer sent a youngster to Ou Nefie for some transaction and he had to hand out change, he pulled out the chest from under his bed, took out the money and always said: "O dear! This is my very last bit of money!"

How wealthy Ou Nefie was, only his attorneys knew and in particular "Pops" Bailey of the firm Pocock and Bailey in Oudtshoorn. But he would never tell.

It is known that Ou Nefie was survived by two married granddaughters whose husbands respected the old man and the inheritance which he left them. The family Wicomb, in particular, did their predecessor proud in their achievements to this day.

Another mountain character who remains alive in the telling was Hennie Alberts.

Most farmers trained *steekbaarde* (whiskered mongrels) to hunt vermin for them. Hennie had two. One day they followed a jackal who disappeared into one of the small limestone caves in the mountain. Hennie waited until nightfall for them to return, but in vain. He kept watch and labourers kept watch round the clock for a full week, but no dogs!

Then, after eight days, one of the animals crawled out of a hole in the Vinknes River bed, thin and weary but alive.

To this day, mountain folk can only guess as to the underground tunnels which this four-legged speleologist had explored and the wonders it might have witnessed.

Most mountain folk believe there is no such thing as working too hard. In fact, most of them lived to a ripe old age and their ages could not be guessed from their appearance.

Children in the pioneering days were expected to work side by side with the labourers from morning until night. They were well cared for, they received food and clothing, and inherited the land when their father died.

Most mountains have their hill-billies. And many a Swartberg hill-billy did a roaring trade in *witblits* (home-made brandy). It was illegal to trade or even distill without a licence. This never bothered the Cango or Swartberg farmers overly. They simply spelt *witblits* A-S-Y-N (vinegar) and sent it by mail coach to whoever had ordered it. Needless to say, the coach driver was not forgotten when "favours" were handed out.

Farmers cared greatly about their animals and when transport riding became the main business of the day, they shod their oxen with "half a shoe". When the going was heavy and the road full of snow, some farmers "socked" their oxen with socks made of animal skin and tied around the leg with a *riempie* (leather thong).

At the turn-off from the Swartberg Pass there is a notice: GAMKASKLOOF, the correct name of The Hell. Many a traveller lands in Prince Albert from Oudtshoorn or the other way round, not knowing this and missing the road.

Not far from the turn-off is an enormous flat stone, perched precariously on a smaller rock-stem, almost like a giant toadstool. One is fearful that its fall is imminent, yet it has been there for as long as people can remember, and remained in position through the heaviest wind storms and earthquakes. How it got there is the mountain's secret.

In the spring and early summer, the mountain is a gigantic natural garden. It is a picture of shapes, sizes and colours. Even in autumn and early winter there are enough flowering shrubs and plants to keep one there for hours on end.

Actually to see the white snow protea is a great privilege. If one knows when and where to find it.

Heather (*Erica foliacea*) abounds. Mountain children loved to string the tiny, pearl-like blossoms on a grass stem to form bracelets and necklaces. Proteas from small to giants, flower in all their splended colours, especially if the mountain has had sufficient early rains. The Chinese lanterns are all over, ready to be popped. The small *sewejaartjies* (Leontonyx) are abundant in a variety of colours and sizes, and make a glorious showing; as do the enormous areas covered by white, pink, yellow and mauve clover blooms interspersed with snow-white bushes seemingly covered in cotton balls. For those who look more closely, there are the small and hardy mountain carnations to be discovered. The banks of the fast-flowing streams are lined with stately white arum lilies and small to tree-size ferns.

High up and deep in the mountain, rock formations are solid. They send water downhill and like the cipher fountains, the water is as clear as crystal. Few people can resist lying down to taste this ice-cold, fresh mountain water.

Buck abound. The *klipspringer* (small buck) are so tame and fearless that they stand on rocks staring at the intruder on their domain. There is a good presence of *reebok* (a deer with a shiny pelt and white, plumed tail). And on a few occasions the terror of the mountains, the leopard, has been spotted sunning himself on a rock high above everyone else.

Snakes are plentiful and the mountain adder, in particular, is feared. Mountainlore links it to the ruins of a tiny stone house near the road.

It is said a Duusman (Dutchman) who ran from "the authorities" died a slow and painful death in the house, after being bitten by a mountain adder.

This fugitive could not find rest for his soul and sometimes when you walk in the mountain you may just feel your hair raising or get an eerie suspicion that someone is following in your footsteps.

On some nights when the wind howls through Wyenek (Wide Neck), you can hear his screaming and agonising struggle with death.

At the end of the twentieth century, you still have to negotiate the dirt road over the Swartberg Pass to get to the Gamkaskloof turn-off. This road was opened in 1963 and named after Dr Otto du Plessis, the then Administrator of the Cape.

It was to have cost £5 000, but when the whole project, including the road in The Hell and the causeway, was completed, the account came to £16 000.

This road — more about it and the road maker later — starts after about 57 km of Swartberg road. After 33 km, you come to a true testing ground for drivers when going down the almost forbidding road to the "floor" of the valley.

It is this stretch that prompted a Belgian tourist to write: "May God be with you when a car approaches".

Woe to the person who attempts it with a caravan in tow. It is extremely difficult for two average vehicles to pass each other. Sections of the road appear to be a cut through the rocks and for long distances there are gaping abysses on the other side.

When heavy rain falls, the water brings stones with it.

Sudden blind turns occur on this rocky downhill with its countless hairpin bends.

In earlier years it happened several times that the Kloovers had to chauffeur a terror-stricken visitor out of the valley after his nerves had given way on the down route.

After zig-zagging your way down, you are in Gamkaskloof.

The road is about 20 km long, and on the widest place the Kloof is about 600 m.

There you look up at rocky mountain slopes falling to a V-shape.

The valley itself is a narrow strip of alluvial soil.

All that remains of once-lucrative farms are neglected orchards, barren mealie lands and wheat fields. There are some remnants of primitive *takkrale* (branch corrals).

The houses are well spaced.

The water runs too low for irrigation purposes and the Kloovers did not have pumps. In any case, the muddy water of the Gamka River was described by a resident, Martiens Snyman, as "edible rather than drinkable".

The river divides the Kloof into two, almost equal, sections: the Bokloof (Upper Kloof) and Onderkloof (Lower Kloof).

The waters which feed the Leeu River and the Dwyka River are usable. But the Kloof is rich in fountains and this is the water the settlers preferred.

In *voortye* the shortest route for pack donkeys crossed over Elandspad. But it was difficult.

Three main routes out of the Kloof were generally used, apart from a few "short cuts".

The nearest town was Calitzdorp, but the main business centre was Prince Albert.

Until the Otto du Plessis road was opened, the Kloovers walked to neighbouring towns.

44

To Calitzdorp they made their way through Smit-se-nek (Smith's Neck) and Wyenek (Wide Neck) or through the Gamka River. After wading through ankle-deep water for hours, the hiker crawled out of the valley to find the outside road to Calitzdorp.

There was a route at Seweweekspoort down Die Leer (The Ladder). This was a much-used route. It is a footpath which rises 900 m and was a challenge even for super-fit and experienced hikers like the Kloovers. One misstep and the climber could fall to his or her death. There is, however, no record of any such mishap.

This route crosses Piet Cordier's farm Kleinberg (Little Mountain). It's hidden at the end of Boplaas in a deep basin against a steep mountainside.

The Cordiers used this route regularly. The route was the reason why Piet Botha, a stock inspector, named Gamkaskloof Die Hel. Or so it is said.

Seweweekspoort is included in Kloof lore.

The name literally means 'seven weeks' gateway'.

Some believe the name is a corruption of Severn Weeks, the name of a governor.

Another knows for a fact that a farmer trekking past in *voortye* got lost in the mountain for seven weeks. Or it came from a stock thief who hid for seven weeks before being arrested. Yet another is sure that Zoar-based Berlin missionary Zerwick's name was corrupted to "Seweweeks".

Die Leer remains formidable and leads to Seweweekspoort. After 12 km it joins the Bosluiskloof road.

When the Gamka Dam was built in 1958, it meant the end of the much-used route criss-crossing the Gamka River known as Suidpoort (Southern Gateway) and Noordpoort (Northern Gateway), or Bopoort to Prince Albert.

Skietkrans is known to all Kloovers. The river makes a dogleg turn at a certain place in the mountain. There are several explanations for the name. One belief is that when strong winds come down the steep Kloof mountainside, they echoe like gunshots. Unsuspecting Kloovers in *voortye* sometimes thought they were being attacked by outsiders. Donkeys carrying heavy loads had to be caught and calmed at this point when shots rang out.

An entrance directly from Calitzdorp leads from Kaffirskloof (thought to be a corruption of Khoi chief David Kiever's name) across the forbidding tops of the Swartberg Mountain. Even donkeys refused to walk this route.

Yet for several members of the Marais family this was no bother. It is said that Lenie Marais many a time tackled it alone, rucksack on her back to go shopping. Sometimes her friend Hester Nel went along.

Gamka River was not only the messenger which brought water, but often livestock too, particularly when there were floods in the Karoo; its catchment area. It happened on occasion that ostriches, goats, sheep even cattle would come drifting into The Hell.

Bopoort, the route to Prince Albert, was mostly used for emergencies. Calitzdorp was accessible through Onderpoort and every new arrival soon learnt that routes differed greatly. There were "paths and footpaths" like the city dweller knows his national roads from the highways.

Chapter three
White Inkommers

When visiting The Hell, it soon becomes obvious why there are so many theories about the first arrivals — in Kloof language, *inkommers*.

The main story concerns a Khoi chief, David Kiever, who supposedly chased the last Bushmen out at gunpoint.

Kiever had a white boy with him, one Danie Hartman of Calitzdorp — captured or kidnapped, that is never told, nor how and where he lived in the Kloof.

That the boy could learn an enormous amount from Kiever and his people is a fact. The Khoi knew the best winter and summer grazing and the proximity to water. They knew what they needed to know about plants; medical, edible or poisonous.

The Khoi's love of animals is legendary and he was prepared to risk his life if an animal was caught in a snowstorm or in some other danger. He knew how to defend himself against jackal, lynx and particularly the wild dogs which roamed the mountains.

Many a time *ouma* Jiedik Cordier, one of the first generation *inkommers*, had to lift her numerous skirts and petticoats and scurry high up into the nearest tree when a horde of these murderous creatures trekked through the valley.

Kiever's men apparently took over thieving and cattle raiding where the Bushmen left off.

Might he have captured Danie on one such raid? But why would he have put his life and dwelling place at risk by kidnapping the boy? Puzzling, indeed!

Danie's nickname was Die Byter (The Biter) because he had such unbelievably strong teeth.

How and when and if he escaped from Kiever is not clear from *voortyd* tales, but he did return to Calitzdorp and his family. It might be that he led them, the first whites, to discover the Kloof.

Zannie and Anita van der Walt, the Nature Conservation officials who moved in to manage the Kloof in 1992, have a theory which links up with an old Cordier family tale.

The fact is the Cape Colony moved its frontier post from Swellendam to Graaf-Reinet in the early nineteenth century. Farmers were part of the trek to Graaff-Reinet and passed Gamkaskloof on the Karoo side.

There are remnants of a cattle kraal with no water or worthwhile grazing in its vicinity. It is thought that it is an old outspan.

There is an unknown person's grave as well — an early *trekker's* (pioneer)?

The Cordiers relate how a party of trekking farmers camped outside the Kloof round about 1820. One night the thirsty and hungry cattle broke out of the primitive kraal and made their way through a ravine to the Gamka River.

The *trekkers* following the spoor discovered the Kloof, found their animals and were delighted with the excellent soil and abundance of water. They "squatted" there.

Another story has it that early colonists (called *Voortrekkers*) moved into Gamkaskloof to escape British rule in the Cape Colony. Many Dutch farmers did not agree with British policies.

Would they have made their presence known by registering?

The first transfer of land was issued to David Petrus Swanepoel. In 1833 he applied for land under the quitrent system.

Baviaanskloof, as the whole place was known, comprised the whole valley with the exception of Ossenberg and Brandberg. It was granted to him by the governor, Sir George Napier, in 1841.

The land surveyor described the Kloof as follows: "East, West, South and North are surrounded by rocks, which make it inaccessible except through the Gamka River bed."

On 15 April 1841 the land was registered to Gerrit Johannes Gouws. Johannes Hendrik Mostert who still has family in the Kloof, bought it in 1875.

Not so long ago, the Mostert family found a medal dated 1690 in a cave. This type of medal was issued by William of Orange to his soldiers. Was a white man there in 1690? Or did marauding Bushmen leave it there?

An early documented visit to Gamkaskloof by Deneys Reitz, son of the President of the Orange Free State who accidentally came upon the Kloof during the Anglo-Boer War (1899—1902), confirms the presence of whites and their living conditions,

Harry Oppenheimer's Brenthurst Library holds the original Dutch Journal in which Reitz tells the tale of his sojourn, but copyright is forbidden and the text may not be used.

This English version of Reitz's book *Commando* differs considerably from the original. After the turn of the century, a few Boers under the command of General Jan Smuts were in the Little Karoo followed by British troups. Reitz and Willem Conradie who spied on the Brits, did not like what they saw; considerable troop movements. The marching colonies made them anxious. They decided to move north across the Swartberg Mountains to the Great Karoo to join General Smuts who was on his way to the western Cape. They tackled the formidable Swart-berg Mountains. Two days' climbing found them at the foot of the mountain where it forms sierras. They sheltered under a crest.

The night was dreadfully cold; too cold to sleep. To make matters worse, a heavy mist descended on them intensifying the cold.

Dawn found them shivering.

The two Boers decided to brave the mountain de-spite the fog and followed a northern route.

Four o'clock that afternoon they left the mist be-hind. About a thousand metres below them lay a long, narrow canyon; the sides, perpendicular cliffs. On the floor of the precipice they spotted a cluster of primitive huts.

Could they be inhabited by natives? They never-theless climbed down to investigate. Their track led through a fissure in the crags and at sunset they were in the valley.

While they walked to the nearest hut, they were surprised by a shaggy giant in buckskin clothes. He spoke a strange, outlandish Dutch.

He was a white man named Cordier who lived with his wife and half-wild children in complete se-clusion in the place named Gamkaskloof.

The two soldiers could hardly believe that Cordier knew everything about them. One of his sons was in the mountains and he knew Boers from Brits by the strange language. Being a child of the mountains he could easily conceal himself.

From conversations it became clear that Cordier's knowledge of the outside world was practically nil.

They spent two more days with this "Swiss fam-ily Robinson" [sic]. They were hospitable. They ate goat's meat and wild honey. When they left, Cordier and his son accompanied them to show them the way. At sundown they took their leave.

In July 1999, Zannie van der Walt received a valuable document written by Reitz detailing his visit to Gamkaskloof. There are substantial differences between this account and the one in *Commando*.

Freely translated from the original Dutch, we pick up the tale where a group of Boer soldiers released a British soldier near Oudtshoorn and afterwards realised that he could use "the telegraph" to summon reinforcements. That is when they took to the mountains.

Reitz became so sick and tired of mountainous surroundings (he was a poor Free Stater who was used to flat land) that he longed for the level Great Karoo. The troops trekked through ravines and saw baboons eating prickly pears. Their deft handling of the fruit by rubbing the tiny thorns off on the ground and then peeling the fruit, impressed the soldiers.

At a Jew's small shop they bought ten tins — the whole stock — of fish and a pound of sweets.

After a long search, they found a passable route.

At another Jew's shop they bought peppermints and condensed milk.

The next morning, *oom* Willie Conradie saw a beautiful horse and a good saddle. And took it.

The horse was unnecessary, but they removed it before the Brits could commandeer it.

A coloured man showed them a footpath over the mountain to Prince Albert. There was a route through Seweweekspoort but also a strong British presence. That was out!

"In the last days," writes Reitz, "we had no news of General Smuts and his men, but we presumed they were in Mossel Bay or Riversdale.

"We could not catch up with them and started climbing the mountains early. It was up and down cliffs with only here and there a short resting period mainly for the sake of the animals," writes Reitz.

A horse fainted on the mountaintop and could not be revived.

The view to the south was breathtaking — mountains and deep, dark canyons. The vague line on the horizon could have been the ocean.

The party was delighted to cross the Swartberg peak and thought it would be downhill all the way. But that was misjudgement on their part. The mountain did not descend directly but consisted of promontories and chasms.

They almost lost heart when they could still not see the longed-for plains of the Great Karoo.

They watched every koppie, ravine and dip where foes might hide. When the sun set, there was a different danger. They could easily fall down the steep krantzes.

They stopped for the night.

Wood was abundant and they made "a great bonfire" to celebrate "the release from the *gramadoelas* (wilds) of Oudtshoorn." They slaughtered a buck, ate their fill, sang songs and swapped stories until late that night.

Albertus van Rooyen "had quite a voice" and he sang English songs, with the rest of the Boers enthusiastically joining in the choruses. Field Cornet Cornelius Brink's forehead and arms were covered in lesions and he told fascinating stories of how he came by them during skirmishes in the Free State.

The next morning, shivering from the cold, the troops kept on hiking at the same level but could not find an opening in the mountain chain to descend. At midday the rain stopped. Reitz recorded: "Beneath us we saw a long narrow kloof, or rather split, surrounded on all sides by mountains and on the other side, Seweweekspoort.

"Below on the bottom of this kloof, we could see a few *pondokkies* (shacks) and thought they belonged to Hottentots who might be able to show us a down route.

"*Oom* Willie Conradie and I left the group and went down. The *pondokkies* belonged to whites. Two families. Mostert and Cordier.

"Only two women were at home, but wouldn't tell us where their menfolk were. When they were convinced we actually were Boers, they sent a youngster to a deep cave under a krantz with a message which brought Mostert and Cordier out.

"A boy of about ten years old had been looking for lost goats in the mountain that morning when he spotted us. He sailed on his stomach through the tall grass, very close to us. He counted us and our horses quite correctly. Then sailed away.

"He reported his observations to his father: that the Brits had crossed the mountains to catch him.

"It appeared several patrols were in the Kloof to catch the fellows after they had supplied Scheepers's men with guns and a wounded Boer, a Mr Moore, was nursed to health by a Kloof family and rejoined Scheepers," Reitz wrote.

Since then, Mostert and Cordier were very cautious, convinced the Brits were after them.

A watch was placed in a tree top and when the Khakis (British) appeared in The Nek of the Kloof, the two vanished in a large cave where they kept a supply of rusks and biltong.

Cordier told Reitz that for 20 years he had lived in this place called The Hell.

"It comprised a narrow strip of ground about 300 yards wide and five or six miles long surrounded by mountains. Only Seweweekspoort had a narrow exit which had to be negotiated single file. No wagon or cart could enter or leave this 'wild spot' and once in five years a stranger from outside might come in 'and disturb the peace'.

"When Cordier married, he brought his wife in on foot across the mountains. Seweweekspoort was not yet a route. Not yet negotiable.

"Three children were born before they ventured out to have them christened. Deneys writes: '*Oom* Willie and I were literally treated on honey beer and other delectables. A goat was slaughtered.'

"Thereafter Cordier led us up a footpath where 'other burghers' waited. A huge fire was made and until midnight *carmonaatjies* (chops, etc.) were barbequed.

"Cordier would not let us go. He wanted to know 'everything' about us.

"In the middle of the night his young son clambered up the cliffs because 'he so dearly wanted to be with the Transvalers'.

"Since my horse had been killed at Leeublad (near Oudtshoorn), I spent the nights sleeping in a wheat sack which I got from Stander and in which I had to fit my whole body to keep warm. Mrs Cordier gave me 'a first-class blanket' so I could almost pass as 'well-to-do'.

"That night Cordier shared my blanket and even though it was not very cold, he shivered all night long. He moaned and groaned so much it was hard to believe that he had spent his whole life in the mountains.

"The following day we rode out following little Cordier, very proud of the faith put in him — down the mountainside towards the *pondokkies* where we spent a few jolly hours with two buckets of honey beer.

"Cordier wanted us to spend a week or more with them. He said there was no danger that the enemy would come into the narrow kloof looking for us.

"Cordier's wife was 'in an interesting condition' and he wanted us to wait a while before he could join us to do 'his bit for his people and his country'.

"We were sorely tempted to accept his invitation because we had honestly earned a rest seeing as we had no more than six to eight hours rest a day from the time we crossed Grootrivier (Orange River) on 2 September. It was November. But *oom* Willie wouldn't hear of this. We must reach the Ceres district! His birthplace.

"We tackled the cliffs. Cordier and his son accompanied us and at sundown we crossed the last mountain before descending to the plains of the Karoo.

"Cordier kept begging us for a gun. As Michiel du Preez had lost his in the mountains the previous day, Cordier decided to look for it. In case he succeeded, we gave him 30 cartridges with which he wanted to 'make life difficult for the English'.

"He said: 'We Kolonialers (Cape Colonials) rebelled Queen Victoria to death and we're going to do the same with old Edward.' He was quite convinced the British queen had died of a broken heart because the Cape rebels had stood up to her.

"I gave him a nice silver top boot which I found in the home of Captain Reid near Aberdeen to give to his wife in memory of our visit." [It is still in the family with great-granddaughter Annetjie Joubert.]

"As we were still high above the plains and the down path was very steep, we stayed there overnight," writes Reitz.

Reitz's journal ends this episode with: "Cordier and his son solemnly took their leave, disappeared down the mountainside and returned home."

This document places a few question marks behind several accepted theories. More than that: much-repeated Klooflore.

The name The Hell was mentioned by Cordier to Reitz in 1901 well before Piet Botha the stock inspector is believed to have referred to Gamkaskloof by that name. And would Cordier have mentioned it if the Kloovers loathed the nickname as much as it is said?

One must also wonder about the English "version" of the book *Commando*. And why do the two manuscripts differ so radically.

The disliked name The Hell may well one day feature below the Gamkaskloof sign in the mountains.

And so too, Hendrik Mostert's disgust at the name will figure in future tales. In the 1970s he received his income tax return addressed to H Mostert, Die Hel, and returned it adding "find out if people in The Hell have to pay taxes."

Whether Kloovers like it or not, the name The Hell is far better known than Gamkaskloof. It has come to stay.

In most Kloof tales there is more than one version of stories, but the origin of the name is not different.

The tale that is generally accepted concerns Piet Botha, a livestock inspector from Calitzdorp, who, during an epidemic in the 1920s, had to inspect the dipping of sheep with scab regularly. This arduous journey he called "a visit to The Hell and back"— particularly in the heat of midsummer. The name rapidly took root mostly outside Gamkaskloof.

Another theory is that the name originated in the winter months when the mountains were aflame with aloes. "It looks like Hellfire," they said. Donkeys and Kloovers were the only living creatures who walked up and down Die Leer. Horses refused. Thus the theory that it was found by chance is credible.

Some families heard from their *voormense* that it was found by commandos who were chasing cattle raiders.

Others know "for a fact" that it was found by hunters who followed the spoor of a wounded buck. Would they be the ones to have determined the in and outgoing routes?

Typical self-ridicule in the Kloof is the tale that it was discovered by poor tax-ridden citizens who wanted to hide where not even the most persistent Receiver of Revenue would find them. And if he did, he would have to slog it out to collect their money.

Families entered the Kloof from several sides, depending on their origins. The first Marais is said to have come in to graze sheep.

Mostert and Marais are the surnames found in Onderplaas.

Every one of the 26 families who lived there for many decades could relate how, but not always when, their *voormense* had come to the valley.

Many believe the first *inkommers* were Cordiers. He was a giant next to his waif-like wife.

Today two graves at the foot of a grey *koppie* (hillock) is perhaps the sole reminder of their residence.

One of the Cordiers who settled in The Hell left for a year to find out whether he might prefer living "outside". He returned.

Both he and his wife said the peace and calm had decided them.

Jantje Jans was a Griqua from Britstown. He had heard of the "peculiar place", came to look and never left.

Like Hendrik the Damara, his wife, a Khoi, wanted to see where her ancestors stayed. They built a neat little home and never considered leaving.

Other stories of the earliest *inkommers* concern a Scots missionary, Emmenis from Zoar, Ladismith, who grazed his cattle in the valley. As he enters tales, he exits without details.

"No! No! No!" another will contradict all these theories.

"The very first people who set foot in the Kloof were horse thieves. The Commandoes tracked them and discovered the Kloof."

Some even know these raiders hijacked trains of wagons which they brought to the foot of the Swartberg Mountain, chased the cattle into The Hell and burnt the wagons thus wiping out all traces of their whereabouts.

Still another knows that a Burger family were the first whites there. Soon after their arrival, four children died and they left.

Booi — his surname forgotten — was another *inkommer*. In those days he made a living selling firewood in surrounding towns.

One day he took his donkeys into The Hell and stayed. "After the rushing around in Prince Albert and Calitzdorp and Oudtshoorn, he preferred the peace and quiet."

There was an Esterhuizen family — bastards — so it is said, who all died during the 1918 Spanish flu epidemic. Their graves and primitive headstones are still there.

The first Mostert came from Graaff-Reinet, according to fireside tales. His task was to get rid of the aggressive Bushmen who murdered and thieved as far as they went. Not only did he have to find these skilled hunters, but also their hiding places and eradicate them. He found the last family in The Hell and ambushed them.

Thereafter the Mosterts settled in Gamkaskloof.

Their descendants are numerous. One of them recalled the day when he scoured the mountains for lost goats and came upon a cave. The clay pots, even the ashes of the last fires, were undisturbed. He felt as if the people might return any minute it was so realistic. He discovered many paintings, including one of a white male on horseback, a gun slung across his shoulder and a dog with him: his forebear?

Annetjie Joubert, who owns several guest houses in Gamkaskloof, is a descendant of both the Mosterts and Cordiers. Her father (Mostert) told her that their first forebear who lived in Gamkaskloof was still a bachelor at the age of 44. He looked for someone to wash and iron his clothes. A 17-year-old girl was recruited.

"He felt sorry for her," the family says, "so he married her."

Legally, she was too young, so they changed her age, but their figure work when changing the date of birth did not fit. They made her younger. So the magistrate refused to marry them and they had to wait until she turned 18.

The Nel family trekked to Gamkaskloof when their daughter Bertha was two years old and her brother a babe in arms. She left in childhood to attend high school.

Bertha recorded her family's story and relates an 18-hour walk from the farm Groenfontein in Calitzdorp. She mentions that her grandfather Hartman "had such powerfully strong teeth that he could bite through two-inch nails." Could this be Danie Hartman who had been captured by Kiever? Or a descendant?

The story of the Nel family trek to Gamkaskloof spells out a major reason for resettlement. The whole family farmed on Groenfontein and there was not enough land for all to make a living. Koot and his family moved to the fertile Gamkaskloof across the Mountain. Lewies Nel followed.

Everything they owned was carried in. Over Elandspad and Wyenek. This route, even without baggage, is formidable.

The Nels walked about 29 miles. Some of the "luggage" included an old-fashioned water mill for milling wheat. It was dismantled at Groenfontein. The heavy millstones were carried by Pietie and Danie who helped their brothers with the trek.

Koot reputedly had a weak heart and below his knee was a hole caused by a thorntree stump when, as a youngster, he fell onto it. But he walked with the rest.

Koot Nel built his house at the entrance to the Kloof. Lewies built his further down. The second house to the right upon entering the Kloof was that of Hendrik Mostert. Half-a-mile further on the left was Stappies (Walkies) Cordier and then followed Piet Mostert's house.

Within one decade, 21 families had settled in Gamkaskloof.

Round the family fires it was told how the Khakis (British soldiers) had followed Boer spies, and the Boers had led them into a trap and shot them; at Elandsgat.

Another Anglo-Boer War story tells of a British general who crossed the mountain and found himself in the Kloof. *Ouma* Mostert was busy doing something at Boplaas when he quietly walked up behind her and greeted her. She had the fright of her life and said her *skrik-rympie* (rhyme said when alarmed) meaning: "God bless you and the devil take you." He misheard The Devil and thought she meant the much-feared (Boer general) De Wet and bolted.

Perhaps it relates to an incident when the Mosterts found a wounded man and took him home. *Ouma* Hessie Mostert took the *kruidjie-roer-my-nie* (touch-me-not = Melianthus) from her medicine box, boiled it and mixed it with herbs, seed pods, and more, and healed him.

The stories of *die karkas* (the carcass) in Gamkaskloof will remain as long as stories are told, even though there is no proof of its existence. And these stories are enhanced everytime a goat herdsman finds bones or skeletons in places where people seldom go.

At Baardgesig-se-Kloof (Beardface's Ravine) there is a ghost. A British one? No-one is sure; what they are sure of, is that they had heard or seen it. So it must be true!

Chapter four

Settling

The *inkommers* set up a transport system which almost became standard procedure.

Carrying furniture developed in a prescribed manner. Two chairs per man, two men per table, two per bed and four per wardrobe depending on the size. What could float down the Gamka River was transported by water, retrieved downstream and carried home.

Women were not expected to carry heavy things. Foodstuffs or a child on the back were their main responsibilities.

Donkeys were worth their weight in gold. They were a huge asset! Pack donkeys carried 45 kg on an easy route down or upstream to Calitzdorp. Crossing Elandspad it was halved. Also at Die Leer. No donkey carried paraffin in case it burnt its skin.

Few Kloof men are without back or shoulder injuries. The lesions came from carrying heavy things like black-iron Dover stoves, wardrobes and millstones.

It is difficult to believe that the enormously heavy millstones were carried on men's shoulders.

Even a *skotskar* (tip-cart) was carried in piecemeal.

And a motor car! The first car in Gamkaskloof was carried in in 1958. It was a Morris V-8. The remains are still to be seen at the guest house of Annetjie and Bennie Joubert; at Annetjie's *oupa* Hendrik Mostert's house.

Five years before the Gamkaskloof road was opened in 1963, a good Samaritan, nine men and four donkeys carried it 15 km through Bopoort.

The first motor car to be brought to Gamkaskloof was a Morris V-8. It was literally carried in on men's shoulders.

(Photograph: *Nongqai*)

Donkeys were worth their weight in gold when it came to transporting heavy loads.

In 1958 Ben van Zyl of Wellington visited the Kloof. He met Martiens Snyman and his little girl who were rounding up donkeys on the mountain slope. He was so moved by the happy little soul who braved the thick shrubs, he offered to *abba* (piggy-back) her.

Martiens invited him to spend the weekend with them and he was most impressed with the hospitality.

Back in Wellington he decided to do something for them. He saw the opportunity when he was in Tulbagh. A very useful Morris, without lights or windscreen and roof was up for sale at £15.

Ben and his twin brother Dirk sent a message to Martiens Snyman that they would bring him a *rydingetjie* (vehicle). He should meet them on 11 October at Boplaas to help carry it in.

The excitement, the organisation and consternation can only be imagined. And the spectacle! Never to be forgotten!

There were five possible routes; paths and footpaths all of them. They chose a downward-sloping route. The car was kept upright throughout.

The first two miles of the donkeycart route before the Poort went reasonably well. Four donkeys pulled and 11 men lifted and pushed up and down rocky slopes, through streams and sand.

A "sand wall about 30 yards high" posed a problem.

Rock bursts were grave obstacles and they had to "turn, measure and fit" through narrow spots before "twisting" the car through.

At Venterskrans the going was extremely difficult. A 200-yard krantz was so rocky that the donkeys were withdrawn. The front wheels were lifted up against the krantz and the back pushed like a wheelbarrow to get it up and over.

Then came the Gamka River bed. Nearly a quarter-of-a mile was driftsand. In the interim they ate, rested and drank coffee which Martiens Snyman's son had brought. There was even "something stronger" to lift the spirits.

Like typical Kloovers, nobody was too serious to pass up a prank.

Piet Cordier slipped a stone, the size of a bread, into Dirk van Zyl's backpack thinking he would find it very soon. They got so busy that it was not noticed. When it eventually fell out of Dirk's bag "everyone could still laugh".

At the entrance to the Kloof they put the car down on the dirt road and cheered and clapped their bloody and torn hands.

Piet Cordier fired seven shots and the Morris was push-started.

A great moment! The first car in Gamkaskloof!

Martiens Snyman behind the wheel of the first car in The Hell, with his wife, Sannie, daughter Anna and Piet Cordier. (Photograph: *Nongqai*)

The Ladder on the west side of the valley. It is 900 metres high and leads to Ladismith. Donkeys could not carry more than 50 in pounds weight when moving out. (Photograph: Paul A. Coetzer)

The Norse watermill on Ouplaas.
(Photograph: Dirk Lilienfeld)

The inside of the Norse watermill.
(Photograph: Paul A. Coetzer)

The fig press when closed. (Photograph: Paul A. Coetzer)

The house of Lenie Marais, always a pillar of strength in Gamkaskloof. Some people swear that she built the whole house herself. (Photograph: Paul A. Coetzer)

Martiens could not wait to get behind the wheel. Twenty years earlier he was an outsider and drove lorries during World War II (1939—1945).

After a bit of pushing this and pulling that, he got the car moving. Martiens's wife Sannie, the little girl Anna and Piet Cordier were passengers. Naturally, the Kloof people were all present to witness the momentous occasion.

When this peculiar thing started making funny noises and moved, some terrified children burst into tears and those who did not run for the safety of their homes, hid behind their mothers' skirts.

Ben and Dirk returned the way they had come. They left to a gun salute after shaking every hand in the Kloof.

Kloovers were all given a turn to ride in the Morris.

It was fun driving up and down the 20 mile road. They could not take it out of the valley: there was no road.

When the car had a problem, there was no know-how and the diagnosis was always: "It's the coil."

Martiens had his own fun and played pranks on unsuspecting friends.

Martiens Snyman — a real joker!

One day high up in the mountains minding the goats, the men were sitting on their haunches as usual when Piet Bêrend said: "You know Martiens Snyman once made me push that thing to get it going.

"I badly wanted to go for my ride so I pushed and pushed until I could push no more. Through sand as deep as this! Uphill! Downhill! I pushed! And what does Martiens say? He says: 'Sorry, man, I forgot to switch it on.' After hours of pushing!"

But back to the first white *inkommers* who arrived more than a century ago.

Whether they came in and then built houses or the other way round, is not certain. But putting up a shelter was a priority.

Houses in Gamkaskloof look much the same as those in surrounding towns: triangular, straight, gabled Cape Dutch cottage style.

Some believe the oldest house in the Valley is that of Johannes Mostert. The one in which Zannie and Anita van der Walt live is the largest and might be the oldest. The next oldest was built by Willem Mostert and became a guest house.

A house was generally placed in the centre of the farmyard.

The size was determined by the available wood. The builder inspected the trees. He could choose between red karee, thorn and wild olive. All had shortish trunks. The taller poplars were planted later.

Foundations comprised stone or raw brick blocks. Walls were made of clay and stone mixed with hay and/or grass, and thoroughly kneaded. Clay was smeared on for a smooth finish.

Walls were 12 to 18 inches thick.

The foundations were up to 12 inches, protruded on three sides of the house but in front they were six feet wide for a stoep or patio. Most houses had two outside doors and several window openings. The woodwork was crude for lack of (or perhaps because of) the available tools. Front and back had stable doors with a top and lower section. Windows were fitted with wooden shutters. Initially, there were no inside doors but openings were curtained off.

Floors consisted of a mixture of clay and cow dung. Sometimes glue from the thorn trees was added. In some cases the *melkbos* (milkweed) milk was boiled with bee's wax and the result was a cementlike shiny surface.

Ceilings were made of thick wooden poles; mostly wild olive and later poplar. On this, a layer of reeds (common or Spanish varieties) was placed and tied firmly in position with strips of thorntree bark.

A thick layer of clay was smeared on top. It was called a *brandsolder* (fireproof ceiling) and formed superb isolation. In winter the house stayed warm longer and in summer, cooler.

Thatch was used for roofing but in "modern times" many were replaced with corrugated iron.

When thatch was scarce, rye straw was cut. In early times it had a long stem. Some builders cut a "type of grass similar to the famous Riversdale reed" at Elandspad, and mixed it with rye.

The thatch was laid generously to withstand the worst elements: hail, wind and rain.

Quite soon they had to cover the roof with chicken mesh against marauding baboons perhaps hopeful of finding grains of wheat. When the baboons left, the roof lay spread all over the yard.

In the early days only one house had a bathroom. Toilets consisted of "squatting behind the kraal wall".

Houses were small. Big ones were unnecessary as most of the living was done outside. Throughout the day the tasks were out of doors, even the family's washing was done in the nearest stream.

Willem and Lenie Marais's house.
Left to right: Hannes van der Walt, Martiens Mostert,
Freek Marais and Isak van Eeden. (Photograph: Dirk Lilienfeld)

Furniture was sparse. Everything had to be carried in. The essentials were there. Every house had
black, wrought-iron pots and pans. There was a din-
ing-table, chairs and sideboard.

Bedrooms had beds and wardrobes, and sometimes a dressing table without a mirror. Mirrors
were separate and small as they were fragile and
difficult to carry.

Almost a century before Martiens Snyman's Morris was carried in, Vaal Johaans Mostert brought in
a *bokwa* (buck-wagon). One day the wheels gave way.
Vaal Johaans walked out to Calitzdorp, across
Wyenek for 18 miles, a further 20 miles to Calitzdorp
and back again rolling in two wheels. Then he went
back for two more.

Kloovers relate how Freek Marais badly wanted a breast plough. He left in the early morning from his house opposite the school. He crossed Smit-se-Nek or it might have been Wyenek on his way to town. He bought his plough, put it on his shoulders and walked. That evening he was back home and the following morning, at dawn, he inspanned the donkeys to do the back-breaking work that he previously had to do single-handedly.

This was progress! It was modern!

Voormense did not dig or plough the field before putting in their crops. The field was cleared, shrubs removed and stacked as a hedge. Then wheat was "thrown out" on the land and the cattle, sheep and donkeys chased around to trample it down.

"And," says a Kloover, "thereafter the crops were left in the care of the Dear Lord!"

Gamkaskloof is an extremely fertile valley. And the farmers enterprising. The brothers Hannes and Piet Mostert were two of the very few farmers in South Africa who grew a particular type of onion seed — the very early Malan-de-Wildt type. The average crop was 30 lb from a bag of bulbs. The Mosterts harvested 40 and sometimes 50 lb per bag. Agriculturists state that Gamkaskloof is also a fruit region *par excellence*. And the sweetness and flavour of the fruit are outstanding features. W C Mostert who, with Hannes and Piet, was a fruit farmer exported as far afield as South West Africa (Namibia today).

One need only have visited Gamkaskloof during the fruit season to see the excellent crops. Branches of the much-sought-after Adams figs along river banks, and the Kakamas yellow cling peach trees carried loads to breaking point.

"You could put a stick in the ground and it would grow and bear fruit," one of the farmers boasted. And he might not have been far from wrong.

Chapter five
Making a living

Everything the Kloovers ate came from their farms. And every member of the household contributed, albeit in small measure.

Little ones gathered sticks for firewood, or helped with the herding of goats, sheep and cows. This they did after school.

Girls were expected to help in the house and they loved to churn the butter. Paraffin tins were used. The cream was poured in and a churn staff carefully inserted. A home-made lid was fitted on top of the tin which stood in icy-cold water, brought in earlier from the fountain.

The kitchen was freed of flies by lighting sulphur which smoked them out. Laboriously the churn was turned until the first crumb of butter formed. The daughter called her mother or grandmother who took over. She carefully gathered the crumbs into a solid lump, then lifted it out of the butter milk which was preserved as a delicacy. The butter was washed with a wooden spatula and all the fluid worked out. Salt was added and worked through again.

The girls helped to "pound" butter as the shaping of butter blocks are called. A damp square of greaseproof paper was cut large enough to cover a pound of butter neatly. A wooden one-pound-size mould, which could be opened on several sides, was filled and airholes were press removed. It was then kept in the coolest place in the house until someone walked out to sell it.

There was a ready market in the outside world for Kloof butter.

Girls also enjoyed the roasting and milling of beans for the coffee which their parents loved.

Threshing season was important and a very busy time in the Kloof. Kloovers helped one another. One family's hands were never sufficient. Wheat had to be cut, threshed and winnowed.

Donkeys held a place of honour in Kloof life. Apart from their other uses, they played an extremely important role at threshing time. When it was time to thresh, every farmer saw to it that his donkeys were fat and fit.

The threshing floor was inspected for hardness. Clay, grit and round river pebbles were brought in and trampled down by the donkeys. The Mostert's threshing floor is still in existence.

Lewies Nel once helped them with the preparation of the floor. They were threshing beans or wheat, Annetjie Joubert (née Mostert) can no longer remember which. She says: "Reeds were tied around the floor and then they were thoroughly plastered down with cow dung.

"We did not have enough dung for such a big floor.

"*Oom* Lewies brought a few bags full. Leafgreen dung.

"Now the children had to run to and fro and fill tin buckets with water from the nearby fountain. In the heat of summer!

"The dung was mixed in the little bucket.

"That day *oom* Lewies grabbed my little bucket in which the dung was mixed, thought it was water and poured it over his head — licking the water as it ran down his face.

"The weather was always most important and at threshing time, more so. The partridges were our best weather prophets. Wind plays a very important role in the winnowing process. As soon as the north-easterly breezes start, the winnowing starts, and every available hand is welcomed.

"Everything goes into action.

"The donkeys are inspanned and they walk round and round the threshing floor trampling the wheat.

"The wind takes the chaff when it is thrown up into the air and the corn fell back.

"The children were ready with reed brooms to sweep up corn which shot out too far.

"Until the last grain of wheat is in the grain bag, there is not a moment to be lost on resting, no matter how much tired muscles ache and yearn for a break," says Annetjie.

In this manner, Kloovers went from farm to farm until all the wheat had been reaped.

Almost all farmers had a water mill and it is hard to imagine that this was carried "piecemeal on human shoulders".

Kloof mills are Norse mills. Some researchers believe the Kloof type was influenced by the Roman or Vitruvian mill which underlies the development of water wheels and the harnessing of water power.

The mechanism is simple.

Each mill is housed in a separate little building not far from the house. It is generally made of wood, reeds or bamboo, and has a pointed thatch roof. At the apex it is about 11 ft high.

From the doorway one sees a hollow in the ground and in it a horizontal ox-wagon wheel, the spokes replaced with slanting boards of wood, four inches wide.

A stream to serve this watermill was diverted to send a strong flow of water through the building.

The water strikes the slanting boards causing the wheel to turn.

From the hub of this wheel, an axle protrudes,

passing through a stone disc or millstone, kept in position by a metal band, maybe a hoop taken from a wagon wheel.

The front portions of the metal band had an opening of about four inches. On top of this stone disc, is a second, similar one attached to the axle. The top disc has a round, six-inch hole and in the top rim is a notch.

Above this contraption is a wooden box with a small round opening at one end. A piece of bamboo protrudes from this and acts as a chute carrying grain into a second box. Both boxes could be regulated by strings attached to them. The lower box had a wooden peg at its base which touched the notch in the top stone disc on every revolution. This caused a smallish amount of grain to fall between the two millstones at every revolution which ground it to flour. This flour fell into a container, usually a hessian bag.

For milling small amounts of flour, the farmers used hand mills called *handsteen*.

On entering a millhouse there was a pervading smell of ground wheat and fresh flour. A misty cloud hung in the air.

The hand of the housewife was evident in every nook and cranny of her home, which she kept spotless. Floors were regularly smeared with cow dung which, it was ascertained, minimised dust.

During the mealie season, the folks allowed themselves some fun. At harvesting time they talked about "the coming mealie ball".

Mealie season was for young and old alike. It was never a hardship for children to go and guard the ripening crops on the field. They kept the baboons at bay and picked some of the nicest mealies, roasted them and plastered them with butter which they had brought along.

Sometimes sweet potatoes were dug up with fingers and nails, and roasted in the ashes.

Mealie leaves were used to fashion dolls, and the mealie beard became hair. Berry juice came in handy to paint the dolls' faces.

The boys made clay houses for the dolls and tended the fires for the mealie braai.

When the mealies were ripe, every available hand was ready to pick them. Two cobs were tied together and hung over scaffolds to dry.

The farmer's wife brought along crumpets dripping with butter and honey.

Ginger beer was offered and sometimes something stronger.

Music-makers brought concertinas and guitars, and while they worked they sang and took time off to *skoffel* (dance). Lewies Nel had "a good voice" and led the singing of folk songs.

If mealie harvesting was a mealie ball, goodness knows what grape harvesting should be called. For some it might have been a binge and a ball but for some a nightmare.

Apart from the well-known uses of hanepoot grapes, it was also time for distilling *witblits/withond/witvuur/witklip/vuurwater* (different names for home-made brandy.)

And similar to the traditions adhered to in other parts of the country where *witblits* was made in *voortye*, Gamkaskloof is rife with *witblits*lore.

Stoffel, according to *blits* legend, was "the wildest of the Cordiers" during *blits* season.

"The Cordiers 'were not shy' to take out their old Sannas (rifle) or Martini-Henry's and shoot at one another. Or at anyone, for that matter." No-one was ever wounded or killed.

Ouma Jiedik Cordier came to the Kloof as a 16-year-old bride. She ended her days alone in her little house. Her sister, *ouma* Hannetjie, also lived alone.

Many were the seasons when *ouma* Jiedik's sons tasted and tasted and tasted again to make sure the brew was just right, that "things became a bit rough".

The wives knew it was time to leave them at their stills, gathered the children and bedding and moved in with *ouma* Jiedik and *ouma* Hannetjie. Shakedown beds were crowded into the tiny houses.

Stoffel was a master at the *witblits* still. It was an art to make the fire neither too large nor too small. The *mos* (fermented grape juice) should be distilled not faster than at about seven (at the utmost nine) "pearls" (as drops were called) per minute, otherwise the *uitloop* (outflow) was not strong enough. If it is faster, it is too weak. If every helper did not know his job, the year's crop was a failure.

When the *naloop* (faints) was finished, the *witblits* was bottled or poured into barrels and hidden.

Then life returned to normal.

Stoffel or one of his brothers would set off to fetch the womanfolk "because we're hungry".

Many families made their own *blits*, like the upper Mosterts, Piet Cordier from Agter-Kleinberg and anyone who had the know-how and a kettle. All without licence.

An entertaining *witblits voortyd* story is about the Prince Albert police who dearly wanted to trap Piet Cordier. But he was always too clever by far.

Then they saw their chance when Prince Albert got a new young constable. No-one in the Kloof knew him or anything about him and the police decided: he's our man; he will catch Piet!

"He dressed in civilian clothing and set out," the story goes.

Die Leer — a twisting, perilous trail. Its like ascending a ladder, hence the name. (Photograph: Pieter A. Coetzer)

"The constable left his horse at the top of Die Leer and laboured down into the Kloof. Found Piet. Introduced himself. And looked helpless, but hopeful.

"He hears that this is the only place where one can get very excellent *witblits*. From *oom* Piet. Would *oom* Piet please sell him only one bottle?

"Piet looks sorry for himself. He had a very bad harvest this year. Not much *blits*. But if the young man would like a little to taste he would gladly pour him some. Not for money. No! No! No! Purely for friendship.

"Piet said much later: 'We have now become such good friends that I have changed my mind. I will, after all, sell you a bottle.'

"The constable beamed. He wanted to return home immediately but Piet wouldn't hear of this. They had to have a few more *doppe* (tots) to celebrate this wonderful new friendship. ·

"And," says the storyteller, "Piet provided him so generously with *doppe* (drinks) that he waddled his way out.

"With that *warm lyf* (inebriated body) he tackled Die Leer. As was Kloof habit, Piet accompanied his guest. He walked behind with another bottle in his bag.

"At the top of Die Leer he took leave of his new friend and quickly swapped bottles.

"Piet waited and waited. Something had to happen. He knew what to expect. Then it came. The summons. To court. What do you plead? Piet refused to plead. Stood his ground. Said the magistrate had to taste it first.

"Eventually 'his honourable' uncorked the bottle and smelled.

"'*Sies, magtag*!' he allegedly yelled, 'this is urine'. Only, he did not use a polite word.

Kloof *witblits*lore is always one-sided. Distillers always outsmart "the law". Once the *dominee* (minister of the church) from Prince Albert, a Dr Marais, sent word that he and his wife would be doing house-calls. Ever considerate, he specified date and time.

"Elder Koorts handled the visit and the couple stayed at his house. Setting off on his first visit, Koorts said: 'Wait a bit! I'm not ready yet! I want to take along half a bottle of *witblits*.'

"The *dominee* was shocked. How could a church councillor take liquor on a religious home-call?

"'*Dominee*, it's for medicinal purposes,' he said.

"They went by car (after the road) as far as they could, but the rest was foot-slogging. Mrs *Dominee* was less fit than her unfit husband and Kleinberg was merciless. Up and down. The dirt road was dry and dusty, and eventually every bone in their bodies ached. Mrs *Dominee's* feet wouldn't move and her spirit was spent.

"'This, *dominee*,' said Koorts, 'is when it's time for some medicine to lift the spirits'."

"They sat down and waited for a draught from the medicine bottle when Koorts discovered that it was empty. Needless to say, they were very dispirited that someone else had been so unspirited. Or maybe he had needed the fortification for his nerves, as *dominees* were not regulars in Die Hel."

There is no devil in The Hell, therefore it was not necessary for a *dominee* to reside there, some will tell you. Or, maybe he is scared to be known as the only *dominee* in Hell. Whatever! The Kloovers spiritual leaders lived in Prince Albert and they did not know them in their daily lives. The *dominee* was regarded as an *inkommer*. An outsider.

The view from the top of Die Leer

Another *dominee* story which does not flatter the Kloovers concerns the time the dominee was due to make his round of calls on a specific day. In Bokloof? Or was it Onderkloof?

The proposed hosts decided it would be an excellent occasion to miss.

They arranged for a community picnic high up in the mountain. Picnic baskets were prepared, ginger beer and "so on!" carried along and off they went.

During the afternoon someone remembered that the *voervark* (porker) had no water or food.

Little Karel was a stick-legged boy, quick on his feet, and he was to go and do the necessary.

He ran in a great hurry to be back where all the fun was.

Karel fed the porker and fetched him water, when a stranger arrived.

"*Oom*, what are you doing here?" he asked.

"Why do you ask, Boetie?" said the *oom*.

"*Oom*, the *dominee* is coming to visit and we're all hiding in the mountain. Come quickly!" he added urgently.

Koot Cordier is another *witblits* legend. His barrel of *witblits* was always hidden in the shade of reed bushes near the dam. Every Kloover knew to stay away because the Cordiers "were not backward at shooting". Children were kept at bay by stories of the enormous snakes and other vermin which lived there.

This did not deter the *blits* lust of some. When Koot was inattentive, a small hole was drilled in the tub and a wheat straw pushed in. A tiny wooden peg concealed the damage, and the outside was sanded and muddied until it looked like the rest.

One day Koot took out a tub, found it to be empty, except the inside looked like a porcupine it was so full of straws.

Karel Cordier can tell many *blits* stories.

At Brandewynsnek many a bottle was broken. Some chaps came from Matjiesvlei. Had a somewhat to drink; only when they went out.

"The last drift to cross is at Griffiesnek. Then the water runs into the Gamka River.

"I once walked there with a bag full of bottles of brandy.

"Those stones are wet. And slippery. We're walking. Walking carefully. Very carefully. *Pa* shouts: "'Walk carefully! You just break my liquor today...!'

"I shout back: 'No, *Pa*!'

"Then my feet slipped and behind me was a huge stone. I fell. The bottles broke! Brother! A thing like that is a Kloover's death sentence. I took fright and to my feet. When I fell, *Pa* threw his *kierie* (walking stick) and caught me behind the neck. There's a narrow neck to cross on the other side. *Pa* wasn't anywhere near that neck when I was already home and sitting in the house. With *Ma*!"

One must wonder if the Kloover's grade of fitness had something to do with their resistence to the influence of *blits*. Particularly when Theo Olwage — an ex-teacher in The Hell — tells the story of the day he and "ou Snyman" returned to the Kloof and "ou Snyman" finished half a bottle of blits. At the first rock crossing he announced: 'I'm not carrying this any further.'

"I waited. Something had to happen. We were still on the way when a storm started threatening from the front. We said: 'We'll have to move! The weather's going to catch us.'

"So we moved. I was 23 years old. The strongest walker went ahead and we all increased our speed. The brandy had no effect on 'ou Snyman'. The first drops started falling. We switched ourselves into 'top gear' and 'ou Snyman' left me so far behind I did not see him again."

Witblits gave two of the Piets their nicknames. Piet Kleindoppie (Small Tot) and Piet Muishond (Mongoose). To Piet Kleindoppie you needed only give a tiny tot and then you got out of his way. A Nel he

80

was! Piet Muishond was my father's stepbrother. They tackled him and fed him *blits* at the still once. But did he budge? He was as tough as a mongoose.

"There was this fellow from whom you could buy *blits* for a shilling a bottle. *Withond*. He filled his tub that night and everyone was there. All the farms were deserted.

"The next day he produced more. Everyone was there again.

"What he made, they finished."

Great-grandfather Hendrik Mostert-Fontein.
(Photograph: *Nongqai*)

"Old Hendrik Mostert farmed on Cordier land. At The Fonteintjie (Little Fountain). One side was planted. He made raisins but some *witblits* on the side. Where the fountain comes out, he dug a hole. His first two *ankers* (a quantity) he put in tubs and buried them there. He filled the ground in cleverly and planted reeds on top so that no-one could detect his *blits*. Not like Cordier! He was far more clever. So he thought.

DIE BRANDWAG ★ Vrydag, 17 Oktober 1942.

Piet Cordier. (Photograph: *Die Brandwag*)

"A family member returned from the war. *Oupa* Piet Cordier even gave him a gold pound because he was so brave.

"Now he was staying with them.

"No-one showed him anything. Or told him anything. He figured it out when '*blits* lust' was on him one night. He drilled a tiny hole in the tub, took a wheat straw... And Hendrik Mostert's blits disappeared like Piet Cordier's. And he too was left with 'a porcupine'."

Those who did not make their own *blits* bought from one who had a kettle.

"Once upon a time," starts another tale, "the Cordiers returned along the Matjiesvlei road passing Klein Gert Cordier's farm. He still had *blits*. He was already in bed wearing only his shortie night gown.

"'Go away, man! I'm in bed and I'm not selling you anything!' he shouted.

"But Cordier wouldn't listen.

"'I won't leave! I'm paying you! If you don't give me my *blits* I'll =&@£! you,' he swore.

"Klein Gert, very vexed, flew out of bed, landed upside down in the fire place and all you could see was *kaalte* (nakedness).

"*Tant* Lenie his wife flew up trying to cover his *kaalte* while she shouted agitatedly: 'You're not to look at him!'

"On the fireplace was a bottle of *blits*. In desperation she grabbed it and gave it to Cordier saying: 'Leave now!'"

Beer was actually the Kloovers' favourite brew. Not *blits*. *Geelbek, karrie, k'rie, heuningbier* (different types of home-brewed beer) was their brew.

One or two cases are known in which prickly pears were used but, generally, it was made of honey or honeycomb.

An old Kloover says: "You see the queen bee becomes broody. Some of the honey is used to build up the comb and feed the young bees.

"The first three days with Queen Bee jelly. A pure juice. Then the pollen is brought in from outside. It's mixed in the honeycomb.

"Come the end of September and the pollen oils are part of the comb. You want that pollen.

"Bee's nests in the Kloof are plentiful and some combs are the size of cartwheels.

"Now you press the comb into your calabash. You take *moerbos* (*Trichodiadema stellatum*) root that you have dried, cut it up and put it in a tobacco bag. Yeast! Pure yeast!

"The difference between *moerbos* and yeast is, *moerbos* fans out. After eight hours it's worked through.

"Now you pour it through a cloth. The sediment is at the bottom.

"When it lies quietly it's ready. Golden yellow from all the pollen! *Geelbek*! Pure *karrie*. It kicks like a mule. But not like *witklip*. Three mugs of k'rie and you talk absolute and pure nonsense."

"Piet Cordier, like the top Mosterts, brewed. Not much *witblits*, but *karrie*.

"The one who spots a hive sends out the word: 'That one's mine.' Sometimes he sells his hive."

Karel Cordier was a courting young man when he "made the acquaintance with *karrie*."

He tells his own story.

"Now I come from Bopoort. A girl lives lower down. I want to court her.

"I pass *oom* Hennie Allers.

"'*Middag, jong*!' (Good afternoon, young man!)," *oom* Hennie greets.

"'*Middag, Oom Hennie*!' I reply.

"I alight from my horse and *oom* Hennie, ever hospitable, says: 'Come and taste this!'

"*Oom* Hennie pours a little from the calabash into a little mug. I taste.

"Wow! It's very nice indeed! My ears are on fire.

"*Oom* Hennie asks: 'Are you going to Agter-Kleinberg?'

"I say: '*Ja, Oom* Hennie!'

"He says: 'Have one more for the road!'

"I do.

"Now I want to leave. I get up one side of the horse and fall down the other. It makes no sense. I try again. The horse stands in the *vlei* (marsh). I mount. *Ek neuk weer af*! (I fall off again.) The horse doesn't move. That was his way.

"Let me just add that beforehand I had bought a new suit and a huge box of chocolates from my sugar bean crop. Cigarettes too. I don't smoke but it looked smart.

"I wake up. On top of the chocolates. It was warm and the chocolates had crushed and melted under me. I look at my clothes. Green as grass. The horse had grazed on the new clover. On the one side I'm browned with chocolate and the other side "grass green" horse's s...!

"Whereto now? I try to mount again but keep falling off.

"I grab the mane. Home!

"Now I have to steal back so that *Ma* doesn't ask what happened to my clothes. There's a small outside room. I slip in and bundle the clothes inside Ma's *lappiesak* (rag or cloth bag). Then to the goat kraal.

"I eventually paid the girl a visit but always worried that she might have seen me that first time."

"Whatever the results of *wingerdgriep* (intoxication) in The Helll, there is no known case of addiction. Licentiousness yes. But only on occasion.

Mainly the Kloovers farmed and did it well. Subsistence farming. Almost everything on their tables came from the land.

Zannie van der Walt says farming then was not like it is today.

Today's farmer works for the bank manager. He has an investment to increase, or debt to pay off. The Kloovers did not have a bank or a bank manager in mind. They hardly knew a bank. Only their stomachs. Ask a Kloover what his crops were and the answer will be: "Everything we could eat. And a bit extra to exchange for clothing and groceries, like sugar and coffee beans."

Know-how came from *voortye*: the making of goat's milk butter, the drying and lying of raisins. Even the distilling of *blits*. Sons did as fathers did.

Not so many years ago a young man returned to the family farm after outside schooling and reported that he had planted potatoes "over there". His father was most upset because the potatoes should have been planted "over here" as always.

Only two houses were built on rocky sites. The others were low-lying and surrounded by shrubs and trees.

The daily life in the Kloof centred round the household. That's where they worked, ate, relaxed and slept.

In most cases the house was surrounded by the yard, vines, fruit trees, a wheat field, mealie land and by a vegetable garden. The pigsty had its place as did the chicken pen.

There were kraals for the stock which grazed on the mountainsides during the day but was brought home for the night protecting them from wild animals.

Academics say the "set-up is the focal point of a micro-cosmos in a physical sense, the main sphere of social interaction for members of every household".

Days and weeks went by during which the family did not leave the farm.

Activities were dictated by the seasons.

Slaughtering time was when meat was needed. Mainly man's work. The biggest *kapater* (castrated goat) was selected and slaughtered during winter.

There were no refrigerators and in the cold months meat lasted longer. The processing of the meat was woman's work.

In winter meat could be *biltong*ed (turned into dried raw meat) but in summer it was problematic, even if the meat was hung under the cool reed ceilings.

Sometimes meat was smoked by hanging it in the chimney.

During *witblits* season the housewife saw to it that she was given her share. She made vinegar for the pickling of meat which was salted, peppered and pickled.

Pork fat was cut in thin strips and hung to dry.

This type of meat was used for *bredies* and *potjie-kos* (types of stew). Pork enhanced the taste. Whether it was cabbage, bean or tomato stew, the final product was always tasty.

To this day, the women from the Kloof prepare delicious food like in *voortye*, in black wrought-iron pots on an open fireplace: pot-roasts, onions and small, browned potatoes.

While the meat is fresh, the ribs were *braaied*.

Flour milled by a cool water mill process tastes different from flour which went through a "warm" mill, the knowledgeable Kloover will tell you. From home-made flour, bread was baked in the *buite-oond* (outside oven) and home-made butter liberally plastered on the warm bread.

With this festive food comes a calabash of sour milk, the milk "jelled" in a single lump. A piece is carefully dished into a mug.

Sometimes the family preferred buttermilk. The housewife knew her family liked enough *frummeltjies* (butter crumbs).

Honey was cut into squares and offered on bread or just plain as sweets. There was a choice between *ghwarrie*, *spekbos* or wild plum honey. When bean soup was on the menu, one could smell it from afar. The onions were fried with chopped bacon before beans were added. Every family member brought firewood. Wherever they went, a few branches were dragged home and left beside the fireplace.

Fires are as hungry for wood as people are for food.

Every child and adult was always on the lookout for beehives. Particularly near Spekboom the chances were good. Or the *ghwarrie* trees. Every goat and donkey herdsman knew where bees' nests in the Kloof and krantzes were to be found.

At Knoetskrans and Baardgesig-se-Kloof the bees really worked hard, but it was impossible to get there.

Bees close to an orchard were left to pollinate the fruit trees.

At the end of the day when everything was done, they supped and did their *boekevat* (Bible reading) and crawled into bed, because their working day starts at four or five o' clock in the morning.

Children had a *skottelwas* (wash in a basin). The older ones helped the little ones.

Sometimes an *ouboet* (older brother) or *ousus* (older sister) could be rough when scouring dirty faces, necks or feet.

Come fruit season, and it was "early to rise". Every capable child's hand had to help in the orchards and it was a wonderfully happy time. Children took out their oldest clothes and raced to be there first.

In the fig orchard they knew to pick carefully because green fig milk could make fingers raw.

Everyone filled a basket and emptied it on the place which *Pa* had prepared earlier. Figs, like peaches, had to be peeled. Everyone lent a hand.

Earlier, all hands brought firewood. It was burnt to coals and the glowing coals put in a large drum. A spoonful of sulphur was strewn on top and the basket with fruit hung in the sulphur fumes, the top covered with a bag or canvas.

The experienced farmer knew that the fruit had to be exposed until it was a light yellow colour. Then it was neatly stacked on prebuilt reed drying platforms or on the flat roof of a house.

Fruit season in the Kloof was noisy. Particularly in the vineyard. The birds protested loudly because they could not get to the grapes. The children shouted, talked and sang while cutting the grapes. And of course, ate until their tummies bulged.

For raisin-making, bunches of grapes were put into reed baskets with handles on two sides. The lye was already boiling in large containers, mostly soap pots. A long stick was pushed through the handles so that two people could carry it and hold it in the boiling lye.

Making lye is another *voortye* art. The *asbossie* (lye bush) was plentiful and was stacked in such a way that it never flamed but smouldered. This ash was mixed with water and boiled to a certain strength. The old folks tested the strength by placing an egg in it. When the egg rose, the mixture was ready.

The fire under this pot was carefully regulated.

The basket full of hanepoot grapes was dipped in the bubbling lye until the skin showed tiny cracks. Then it was taken out and dipped into cold water.

A lye-tub used for raisin-making. (Photograph: Dirk Lilienfeld)

89

Beforehand, the children had removed all bad grapes and the bunches were ready to dry to become lovely sweet raisins.

Some grapes were left for making *witblits*. And if the men made *blits* for their own purposes, the housewife claimed her quota. Her home medicine chest had to be filled with *naeltjie brandewyn* (clove brandy) *boegoebrandewyn* (buchu brandy) and *gemmerbrandewyn* (ginger brandy). These were life-savers.

Coffee roasting was girls' work. From *Ma* the daughter learnt the difference between good and inferior coffee beans. Some people added the dried skin of wild fig, called *witgatwildevy*, rye, wheat or dried carrots. The difference in taste was clearly no-ticeable.

The girls helped to make jam and preserve fruit. Every girl knew how to keep a home neat and tidy. The children cared for the animals, raised chickens and collected the eggs.

While the housewife did her chores of washing at the nearby stream, ironing and caring for the house and children, she could adapt her routine to suit herself. There was seldom any pressure on her. The season dictated what was needed.

The man had even less pressure in his chores. The season demanded that he plough, prune, sow or plant. When he ploughed, he used his donkeys.

With the help of his sons, the goats and sheep were released from the kraal in the morning. All day long the mountainside was dotted with grazing animals. Late afternoon they were brought back to the kraal.

Farms mostly had two small fields below the house near a water furrow. Some fields were irri-gated daily.

After the fruit harvesting, every family member kept an eye on the drying process.

The Kloover of old had little need for socialising like Outsiders know it. He was part of nature, knew the seasons, fruits, watering places and cool spots, and enjoyed them all.

Even the children, when seriously questioned, talked of the isolated days as "happy ones".

Few things were so urgent that they could not wait a while.

If the father tired of one task, he could switch to another. Like going up a kloof to chop firewood. Or coming home for a coffee break and sitting in the kitchen with his wife.

Or he took his gun when collecting goats, sheep or donkeys, in case there "was something to shoot for the pot". Maybe a *steenbok* (small antelope) or a wild goose.

Children went to school in the morning. In the afternoons they played separately or in groups. The river and water furrows were favourites. Here crabs could be caught. Or they shot small birds with their *ketties* (sling shots). Even when rounding up animals they played as they went. Late afternoon was generally family hour. The children were back in the house while *Ma* prepared supper. *Pa* sat on the stoep. In the warm months he enjoyed the evening breeze while smoking his pipe. Otherwise a huge fire was made and the stories, mostly starting with the words: "*In die voortye...*" were told. Family histories and stories were preserved in this manner and ties with the past confirmed over and over again. Families enjoyed singing.

Riddles were asked. A typical Kloof riddle would be: "Which rock do you find under the water?" The answer: "A wet one." Or: "Why did the baboon run across the mountain?" "Because he couldn't run through it."

One Kloof story is reminiscent of Til Eulenspiegel. It tells of a young man who badly wanted a donkey.

One day he passed a pumpkin field and saw a baby donkey. He concluded that pumpkins were donkey eggs.

For days he sat on a pumpkin to breed a little donkey.

Then he got hungry. He went home to eat and when he returned, a rabbit was eating a hole in his pumpkin. When the youngster approached him, the rabbit ran away. "Come back!" he shouted. "Come back! I'm your *mamma*!"

Fireside tales were also used educationally. Children were kept in check with scary stories.

Forbid an adventurous youngster to do something and it is an invitation to disobey mischievously. So children were frightened away from dangerous places because there "are evil spirits". Like at Baardgesig-se-Kloof. Like Bushmen girls were terrified of lightning, Kloof girls and boys were told that "the *bliksemstrale* (lightning bolts) hit there more than at any other place, because of evil spirits."

And as proof that the spirits or ghosts were there, children were told how "dogs sometimes tackled absolutely nothing, barking and going wild and biting at seemingly thin air."

"The dead must be left alone," the old folks said and dangerous places were reputed to be the last resting place of "people who spook there."

So impressive were these tales, that many a child confessed at the fireside chats how they actually heard the ghost. And when twigs cracked or a startled bird flew up, children sometimes came racing home.

Few children knew much if anything about the outside world. They loved hearing about shops and the things in them. Social calls were mostly made to relatives.

Fishing was a favourite Kloof outdoor activity.

Kloovers sometimes used a type of fish trap, a funnel made of chicken wire, in the Gamka River. The fish could swim in but not out. The trap was anchored by a large stone and the anchor line covered with stones.

Lots of *moddervis* (mudfish) were caught.

Kloovers made a particular delicacy of eels.

The fish which was not eaten fresh was either pickled or dried. Fish grilled on the coals was a favourite. Sometimes it was hung in the chimney and smoked.

A typical visit to the fishing waters would be between the families of Henk and Koot Cordier.

The men grouped together and drank *karrie*. Wives chatted and the children played.

Then the men got busy dragging nets and pulling out fish. The women cut up and prepared the fish.

In the late afternoon a large fire was built at one or the other's house, fish grilled and the rest shared.

Similar visits occurred spontaneously when someone's roof was rebuilt, or a room added. Everyone helped.

It was not as though the task could not be handled by the family, but Kloover's were always ready to lend a hand.

The day mostly ended late in the afternoon or early evening, round a bonfire and families shared one another's *voortyd* stories.

Chapter six
Coming and going

How many people can distinguish one donkey from another? Don't they all look alike? Like donkeys?

Baroness Thatcher coined the phrase: "A cow, is a cow, is a cow."

If she had said: "A donkey, is a donkey, is a donkey," the Kloovers would have laughed at her.

Each Kloover knows his donkeys individually.

Hundreds of donkeys graze on the mountain slopes until they are needed. Then fathers and children go up and down fetching their animals. Easily 300 altogether. Each one knows his own.

Oom Lewies finds his ten. The Marais find their team. Schalk Joosop and Jan Andries catch theirs, about 25 altogether, and Freek Marais misses one of his. They help one another until the teams are completed.

A donkey is a prized possession. He conveys goods. He is a draught animal and essential worker.

Marina Nortier (née Ehlers) found out soon enough when she was appointed teacher in The Hell that a donkey was indispensable to keep her independent when she wanted to go out to visit and return.

During the reaping season, donkeys are essential. Crops can easily total 15 to 20 donkey loads.

Donkey sagas are seen in a different perspective when Karel Cordier gets talking.

"You see they grow up *geil* (wildish) in the mountains. All of them with black-and-white potbellies.

"One day a Van der Bank chap wanted to buy one. They walked three days. All over Gamkaskloof. They found the donkey near Kliphuisvlei. Way over theeere! There's no road. That's where the donkey is.

"Next day, some Kloovers come to help them.

"The third day they've got him!

"This donkey had straight hair. Flacid. When he runs, his hair is straight behind him.

"He catches the donkey with an *osriem* (ox-reim) around the neck.

"*Pa* gives him *padkos* (provisions).

"*Pa* says to him: 'Giel, you have to climb Bo'jaanskop (Baboon's Hillock) where Hans Joubert lived; where I found the hole where wind comes out.'

"The bloke leaves for Matjiesvlei. There's no food at Matjiesvlei.

"They even buy their bread from the Kloovers. So *Ma* also gives him some *padkos*.

"He walks. Over Bo'jaanskop. He's on top of the Swartberg. He wants to eat his *padkos*. He opens the paper bag. The thing rustles. And frightens the donkey.

"Old Giel had the reim round his hand and the galloping donkey drags him to the cliff edge. Just in time Giel frees himself.

"The donkey can't see. Blinkers! Now he runs along the cliff edge. Giel watches from the top. That donkey falls! And he falls! Onto the rocks in Kliphuisvlei where he lands on his feet. And the donkey runs away. The *osriem* in a straight line behind him. Up to Withoek.

"And there that donkey stayed until the harness rotted off. Never to be seen again. Only heard. Sometimes a familiar grunt could be heard!"

Donkeys were indispensable to the Kloovers.
Each one was known individually to its owner.

Koot Cordier recalls another incident about Michael
and Stryker, two trained donkeys, and the time his
ma sent them to fetch flour at their *Omie* (uncle)
Piet's mill. For making milk tart for New Year's.

"We load half a bag of flour on each donkey. Now
we want to go out. We tie a rope around their bellies
and the flour. I'm in front and Karel behind. I have
to keep the donkeys from 'jump starting'. Stryker
thought otherwise. I try to control him. I grab him
by the tail and that's when he flies away knocking
me flying too.

"I couldn't see a thing. Round me and over me
everything is snow-snow white. Flour where you
look. All the way down the road to the first house.
There's a gate. That's where we end up with the two
bags. Practically shredded. Where are we going to
find our New Year's milk tart?

96

Antiquated school desks. (Photograph: Paul A. Coetzer)

The school on Middelplaas was built in 1928. It was also used as a church and was closed early in the Eighties. (Photograph: Paul A. Coetzer)

The Gamkaspoort Dam which was completed in 1969. The dam obliterated the exit route to Prins Albert. (Photograph: Paul A. Coetzer)

The airport runway was approximately 260 yards in length. Doctor Manie Coetzee used it as a landing strip for his Tiger Moth when he came to attend to the ill. It was a difficult and dangerous exercise. He, therefore, only treated emergency cases. (Photograph: Paul A. Coetzer)

vi

"Old Michael had a little bit left.

"Much later we caught Stryker. And the bags. Tatters. Nothing left.

"That evening we had to use the *handsteen* (hand stone) to grind half a bag of wheat. And we had to hurry because it was almost New Year. We ground. The next day in the warm weather we ground until the sweat poured down."

Koot ends his story in typical Kloof style: "We got our New Year!"

The Cordiers who lived near Die Leer witnessed numerous loads going up those treacherous slopes to the world outside.

One such case was during World War II. Lots of jam was needed for the soldiers in the north and overseas, and Gert Pretorius of Calitzdorp sold the Kloover's fruit crops for them.

S A Dried Fruit Company of Worcester bought it from him.

Once a week during the season he took a family member along to buy figs. On Wednesday mornings they would leave Calitzdorp and in the afternoon they were at Die Leer.

"We crossed the river at least 30 times at causeways," Gert remembers. This they did in their bakkie, which they left at the top.

"Going down Die Leer there's a place where voices carry well and they regularly shouted: "'*Oom* Piet! (uncle Piet Cordier) *Hou die koffie reg*!' (Keep the coffee ready.)

"Then Piet yells back: 'Come along fellows! We're waiting!'

One day the magistrate of Calitzdorp came along to see what Gamkaskloof looked like. When Gert announced his arrival he shouted to Piet: "The magistrate is with me for the dog tax!"

When they arrived there were no dogs in Gamkaskloof. Only when Gert admitted to the prank did the children return from their hiding places in "instalments" with a dog or two on a leash.

On the Wednesday evenings of Gert's visit they socialised. The figs were picked beforehand.

Around the fire all the news was shared. *Tant* Sannie Cordier received newspapers and magazines which she devoured.

Someone remembers: "One of the Mosterts, I think Hannes, after cars came but before the road, saw a way to help Kloovers and make some money for himself.

"Where Gamka Dam is today, was his station. He built a 'tin house' and bought a Diamond T-truck. He would meet Kloovers there and dispatched their goods which had to go by train, seed or dried fruit, for them at a fee. He was prepared to taxi Kloovers to their venues.

"However, most Kloovers believed that riding was not for people with sturdy legs and feet, and a body. They walked."

When going out with healthy donkeys, they timed the trip so that the animals were not caught in Die Poort at night time. The much-feared *tiers* (leopards) and wild dogs kept there.

For a child to be allowed to go out with a parent was a great favour and adventure. Weeks beforehand they looked forward to the trip.

Before the excursion, every weather report on the radio was monitored. Particularly that of the Great Karoo; the catchment area of the Gamka River. Rain decided times of business.

The Gamka River could be very dangerous when in spate. Even with normal rains it was difficult to cross, as the water was muddy and the stones to step on not clearly visible. The visible ones were slippery.

If business was urgent and the river was in spate, the Klippiesvlei route was followed over Doringkloof road. The road was not distinguishable everywhere.

On such a trip *padkos* was inevitable. So too were fresh bread and honey, cold meats and buttermilk. And every child will tell you that *padkos* was much nicer than the same food ate at home.

Sometimes they saw a *ribbok* with its plumed tail or shiny *klipspringers* which were plentiful as their meat was unappetising. Everything along the road was noticed so that the children could tell *Ma* about them when they returned.

Prince Albert was "a huge place" and the children's eyes bulged when they saw the traffic and so many people and the clothes they wore. They listened dumbfounded to the conversations.

"At the shop — if that was possible — their eyes bulged even more. In the odd magazine which the teacher brought, they saw pictures of things like toothbrushes and toothpaste. At home they used powdered ash from the fireplace mixed with fine salt in which a square of flannel over the finger was dipped and teeth cleaned.

"*Pa* talks. And exchanges. This for that and that for this. The children get sweets from the storekeeper on a good day. And believe it or not, *Pa* buys a bottle of scent for *Ma*.

"The road back home seems forever. There are so many things to tell *Ma*."

Another Kloof saga of "going out" is recalled by Annetjie Joubert.

"One day *oom* Oubaas Botes took off with a basket of eggs behind his back to Matjiesvlei, to barter.

"He had a way of carrying his *kierie* (walking stick) in the crook of his arm when lighting his pipe. Everyone warned him that one day he would trip himself with the walking stick. But he would not listen.

"Now let me tell you, you have to know Onderstepoort to walk it. Even without eggs on your back, it's not child's play.

"This day he carried 44 dozen eggs on his back. He walks through the Kloof. On through Die Poort. He crosses Wiel-se-Boud safely, then Helpmekaar, Brandewyngat where you have to be very cautious, and down the krantz into the hole where *witblits* drinkers finish the last drop if they do not want the bottle broken. Then to Bakkrans and Koningin-se-Gat, where you cannot get out if the wind blows. You lose your balance and you will fall into the water-hole. Griffiesnek you cannot cross at all. Not with eggs. You have to follow the level routes and use the stepping stones to cross.

"*Oom* Oubaas does all this expertly and safely. Five hundred and twenty eight eggs on his back. He wants his pipe. Badly. Then the thing everyone predicted happens. His kierie in the crook of his arm lands between his legs and trips him. There he goes. He rolls. And rolls.

"He gets up. He's yellow. Covered in egg yolks. He takes the basket off his back. Opens it. One single egg whole!"

"The Mostert children — Piet's family — had to return to school after the midyear holiday. They had never used the Wyenek route. Terrible streams of water," remembers Annetjie Joubert (née Mostert) who had to start secondary school. "The river flows strongly. I have to get there, river or not!

"The Nel children also have to go to school. Groenfontein farm school.

"*Oom* Lewies Nel comes along. He sometimes carried his small children in bags out of the Kloof.

"Now my *pappie* (daddy) says to *oom* Lewies: 'Lewies, they're quite a lot of girls. Their *voetegoed* (shoes) are not so good'. The school cases are made of cardboard with a handle.

"I'm very independent. I refuse to carry it on my back. I carry it in my hand.

"We walk. And we walk.

100

"Pappie asks: 'Lewies, can we go on with the children? Look at the weather!' *Oom* Lewies was chewing tobacco and he spits in an arc. *Oom* Lewies was a soothsayer. Like aunt Betjie. She was married to *oom* Johaans. Red Johaans? No! I think to black Johaans.

"*Oom* Lewies spits a stream of tobacco juice. 'Listen, Piet! When that bird sings, the rain is gone.'

"We carry on. Lewies leads. It starts raining. We start the uphill out of Gamkaskloof and the fog sets in.

"We walked from eleven in the morning. My *voetegoed* gives up the ghost. My suitcase collapses. I hang on to the handle and my pride.

"Pappie has a sack of potatoes on his back. He ditches them and gives me the bag.

"Eight o'clock that evening we're at Groenfontein. I remember a lovely hot bath and delicious warm food.

"Then the heavens truly opens. The river comes down in spate. We're trapped. For days on end."

Annetjie concludes the story: "I eventually got to school and we're all educated in spite of the weather."

Kloovers recall another story about the Nels and school.

Koot Nel — with the hole in his leg — died in the 1940s. Aunt Hessie, his wife, was left with nine children. For three years and three months she coped alone. Then she had to move to Matjiesvlei and stayed where the Gamka River comes out of the Swartberg Mountain. Her little house was a true haven for every Kloover who was stranded and had to stay over. Koot died at the end of October.

Before his death, they had decided that the children had to complete primary school in the Kloof and then had to go out. Their daughter Bertha had to go to a Domestic Science school at George.

"He died when Bertha was in Standard Six," Kloovers recall. "Even with nine children, her plucky

mother never considered that her children's schooling should end prematurely.

"One morning aunt Hessie said: 'Bertha, you and
Ria (the three-month-old baby) and I, all three of
us, will go to Prince Albert on Friday. After school.'

"She wanted the application forms for Bertha's
school. And old doctor Van Wyk to examine her
properly.

"Aunt Hessie wanted to know what goes for
what," they say. She was a thorough woman.

"Friday after midnight they left the Kloof. Along
the way, the other children were dropped off at
Lenie Marais's.

"They took the *langpad* (long road). On foot. From
Elandspad down through Bopoort to Prince Albert.
Thirty-six kilometres.

"They're carrying a baby, a handbasket with food
and a dilapidated suitcase in which to carry school
clothes they had to buy from the Jew's shop. The
money was not enough to include a new suitcase."

Similar tales about how Kloof children were educated abound. With an enviable doggedness, they
literally and figuratively made their way. The earliest *Inkommers* — after the whites had chased out the
Bushmen, were the Khoi. They came in to collect
honey from bee's nests. This, the Cordiers did not
like at all. With hawk's eyes which missed nothing,
they watched every movement on the mountains
and eventually pinpointed the honeyseekers.

The Cordiers regularly visited their own nests to
see which were ready to be harvested. And they
staked them out with a gun in hand. As soon as the
Khoi came in, two shots were fired against the
rockface just above their heads. Whether this cured
their lust for honey no-one knows. Maybe they chose
life above honey.

An old, old story which no-one can confirm and
which everyone tells is that *inkommers* were not wel-

come in the valley. Particularly those who asked for work. A story of how they got lost is also told.

One such stray arrived on a fine day — and the name and place differ depending on who tells the story — to ask for something to eat. He was lost, exhausted and famished.

He was given bread and goat's milk.

"Can you work?" the farmer asked. The stray was not only willing but "will do anything wherever he is needed."

He cleared the fields. Helped to stack thorn kraal walls. Caught donkeys, inspanned them, ploughed the land, planted seeds and made irrigation furrows.

The tall yellow man with the straight black hair worked from early morning until late at night.

"Six months. Then he announced: 'I have finished! I want to move on.'

"The farmer, as was usual, carried his gun with him. He gave him a lift on his horse to Bopoort, all his worldly belongings on his back. At Bopoort one shot rang out.

"The farmer returned. And he tells you there's a new hole: Jan-se-gat (Jan's hole). That is in addition to all the others: Piet-se-gat, Koos-se-gat, Hans-se-gat, etc."

Many Kloovers suspect Koot Cordier of being the originator of these and similar horribly unflattering Kloof stories. He could keep a straight face and tell such tales to gullible strangers. At Prince Albert and Calitzdorp where he shopped, tall tales were regularly told and later repeated as gospel.

Shortly before his death at the end of 1998, Koot told of the *inkommer* and how he — Koot — inspanned the man and forced him to plough the field all day long and then he took him to the Poort and got rid of him in one of the water-holes which he called Stoffel-se-gat.

Chapter seven
Life-savers

Every town, village and settlement has its medical legends. Gamkaskloof is no different.

Doctors were fetched only in a life or death situation, otherwise they had their Sannie Cordiers, Hessie Mosterts and Lenie Marais's. Add to that: every housewife had her own medicine chest and the "nurse", in fact a midwife, was only summoned when the housewife could not cope.

Sannie Cordier was a legend in the Kloof. Not only was she a good nurse but a trusted midwife and advisor and Kleinberg was no obstacle when she was needed.

Many was the time that she returned dogtired and wet with perspiration from a sick bed when another patient waited at her home.

Of *tant* Sannie the Kloovers say: "When she entered a room your heart opened up again."

Having said this, they also scolded her if she did not hurry.

Tant Sannie's "little black bag" was an old-fashioned *trommeltjie* (small trunk). Full of magic potions. Things like *getrekte ysterbossie* (extract of Dodonaea viscosa) for influenza; and grease and terpentine plaster for inflammation, and if the patient's chest cold turned nasty, the unfortunate domestic cat had to be sacrificed and the warm skin put on the patient's chest, to save a life.

There were remedies for practically anything that hurt or made people ill.

A baby's mouth thrush was cured by mixing the juice of the succulent *ghoukoms/hotnotsvygies/goena- vye* (Hottentot fig) also called *suurvye* (sour fig) and mixing it with Epsom salts to wipe the inside of the mouth using a new *flennie lappie* (flannel cloth). Or *ghoukoms* mixed with aniseed. A weak saline solution mixed with finely ground *dassiepis* (hyraceum) was used to bathe a feeding mother's breasts. The skin was kept supple with a rub-down of sweet oil.

Aniseed water was given to colicky babies.

Septic sores were healed with young peach leaves made into a "paste" with some *dassiepis*. This ointment was put on a flennelet and tied on the sore with a strip of cloth.

For septic scratches and sores, a paste was made of *komynbossie* (cumin shrub) using the leaves and stems only. *Getrekte wildeals* (extract of wormwood) is added. Or karee (Rhus lancea) leaves. All alleviated pain. For angina, *Hotnotskooigoed* (Helichrysum crispum) was drawn to a strong "tea" and mixed with *rooi laventel* (red lavender — a Dutch remedy). For toothache there was nothing to match the young leaves of the karee tree. A handful was picked and chewed.

For cold sores (herpes), karee leaves were boiled, left to draw and the sores washed.

Kloovers were walkers. Foot problems were inevitable. *Soutslaai* (ice plant) was boiled and left to draw and mixed with Epsom salts. Tired, aching feet were soaked in this mixture.

Inflammation was a serious illness. Wagon grease was mixed with cattle dung and peach leaves, first bruised and then boiled.

It was spread on a *flennie lappie* and put on the inflamed area.

Youngsters, particularly, were sensitive about warts and similar growths. The wise old women knew that the milk of a green fig or fig leaf removed it after several applications.

Sore eyes were bathed in *blousel* (laundry blue). Otherwise it was wiped with the patient's own urine on a *flennie lappie*. A drop of castor oil was then added to "break the inflammation".

Very few Kloof children went without garlic tied around their neck. It guarded them against many illnesses.

Tant Lenie Marais was also a specialist in her own right. She helped wherever she was needed. Like most Kloovers, she had her *ouma* (grandmother) and her *oumagrootjie's* (great-grandmother's) knowledge of folk medicine, but she also knew how to brew potions. She owned several Hollander's Home Doctor guides. She probably learnt about anatomy from these medical books as she had a thorough knowledge of things like possible complications at child birth and how to prevent, or handle them. In 1948 the Kloof school had its first-ever visit by a school nurse.

Sister Sarie Röhm was the health authority in charge of schools, and her records showed that no visit had ever been made to the school in Gamkaskloof.

"This situation had to be remedied," the conscientious woman decided. Like other medics, she soon learnt that nothing, if anything, was known about the health of people in that desolate valley.

Colleagues tried to intimidate her. "When a doctor is called, they bring a donkey to Die Leer. And when there isn't one tame enough, the men carry him for eight miles in the river-bed," they said.

However, Sarie Röhm was not only conscientious but courageous. She went to the police station where she arranged to accompany the constables on their next routine inspection trip to Gamkaskloof.

This happened so quickly that there was no time to notify the Kloovers and she also realised there would be no transport and the whole trip would be on foot.

Constables Van Wyk and Viljoen drove to the entrance of Die Poort. From there they walked. They carried rucksacks and guns and she her medical bag.

"The route became increasingly difficult," she later recalled. "In the river the men jumped from stone to stone, but by then my legs were so stiff and sore that I could hardly raise my feet to walk. I walked the eight miles through the river, shoes and all. I dared not rest because that would intensify the stiffness.

"After what seemed like a lifetime — about midday — we left the shady section and walked in the searing sun, a further three miles to the nearest farm house.

"Even though they did not expect us, we were invited to join them for a lunch of meat, potatoes and mealie rice.

"We learnt that the school day ended at half past twelve. We had to let the teacher know immediately that all the children had to return at half past two.

"The school comprised one classroom and a retired teacher, Mrs Joubert, was in charge.

"Although the children were a bit cagey, they allowed me to examine them thoroughly.

"To my surprise, I found that quite a number had enlarged goiters. Probably caused by a lack of iodine in the Kloof's water. I arranged that codliver sweets and iodised salt be sent to the Kloof.

"Andries Marais was chairman of the school committee and I spent the night at his family home.

"I realised that in spite of the skills — Mrs Marais did beautiful needlework which I admired — these people would not easily fit into the world outside their valley.

"The following day, very stiff and very sore, I went back the way I had come.

"The visit," she concludes "was well worth the effort. After a few days in bed."

The most memorable medical happening in Gamkaskloof occurred in the late 1940s, early 1950s.

Dr Garisch of Ladismith was still a young doctor in partnership with Dr Blyth.

He had had a very busy and trying day. It was his usual Thursday clinic at Zoar, a settlement, with every one of about a hundred patients wanting medicine. He always carried a "special Zoar medical bag" on these days.

"After such a day one is exhausted and the fuses a bit short," he admits. He had just arrived home when the telephone rang. "Doctor, would you please go to Gamkaskloof? As soon as possible. There's a very seriously ill woman who needs treatment urgently," the caller said.

He knew it would be a matter of life and death. He was told that the Gamka River was in flood. The regular Kloof doctor from Prince Albert could not cross the river. Which also applied to the doctor in Calitzdorp. The one in Laingsburg did not see his way clear to go.

Dr Garisch, considering that his partner was not well, decided he simply had to go. What if the woman died?

He had no indication of her illness. What sort of medicine should he take? Once there, there was no returning to his surgery.

That was when he thought of asking one of the sisters at the hospital if she would accompany him. Two heads are better than one. Sister Van der Berg of Opsoek agreed to go.

The message which Dr Garisch got was that one

of the Cordier men would bring a horse to the foot of Die Leer.

They only realised how dreadful conditions were when they arrived at Bosluiskloof pass. The turn-off was completely washed away and they had to guess a route for at least six miles, before they arrived at the top of Die Leer. It was pitch dark by then and they negotiated this dangerous climb in torch light.

Cordier was waiting with an extra horse.

The first problem arose. There was only one spare horse as no-one had informed them of the sister's presence. Cordier couldn't walk uphill as he got severe chest pains. "Typical of angina pectoris," the doctor realised. Sister van der Berg was given the horse and the doctor walked.

They crossed Kleinberg (Small Mountain) which was not so small and then walked for miles and miles on the banks of the Gamka River where a cart and horse waited to take them through a negotiable spot in the river.

At half past one in the morning they arrived at the home of the local teacher, Sankie Marais. The patient.

Dr Garisch was horrified when he saw her. The tip of her head and her heels were all that touched the bed. Her body was bent, taught like a bow string.

"I got a feeling of total dejection and hopelessness when I saw her," he admits. "This meant only one thing, an advanced and serious case of tetanus. And in those days the prognosis was zero.

"I simply could and would not believe, however, that all our effort and the stress and strain to get there were to no avail.

"Tetanus is caused by germs which live in the absence of oxygen, generally in decomposed organic material somewhere deepset in tissue.

"Such a wound has to be found and cleaned immediately with peroxide or hydrogen. If not, toxins keep forming and the spasms which contract the muscles, continue.

"Eventually, they cause spasms in the breathing muscles in the chest diaphragm, which cannot function.

"What makes it more tragic is that, throughout, the brain is hyperactive and alert, and the patient cannot relax or rest.

"What could I do in such dire circumstances?" he asked himself. "I simply closed my eyes and prayed to God in his great mercy to give me wisdom.

"Then I started looking for the cause. It took a minute or two before I found a long, rotting thorn in the hollow of her foot.

"It was obvious the patient could not remain in the Kloof. The slightest movement caused a severe spasm.

"How on earth were we going to get her to a hospital? In Ladismith! To carry her across the mountain was impossible. To take her up Die Leer impossible. The river was in spate but that was the only alternative. Could she be carried along the banks where possible and the rest of the way through the river?"

His thoughts raced on. "How do you transport such a seriously ill person. There was no such thing as a stretcher. Perhaps the frame of a single bed. Is there one? No! Kloovers have only double beds. Then someone remember that on a small farm some 12 miles away there and back there might be a single bed.

"What about bearers?

"I was determined that every possible human effort had to be made to save the patient. Once more I

Life-savers

prayed for wisdom and strength, and then left things in the hands of the Good Lord.

"I told the family it was in their hands to find enough bearers.

"I gave the patient a morphine injection and dog-tired, I lay down to rest for a while.

"When I opened my eyes a bit later there were eight men with a single bed frame. They arranged that four to a team would carry Sankie Marais and that they would keep to the river bank as best they could. For the rest they would lift the patient waist-high and even shoulder-high through the river.

"Sister Van der Berg and I would return the way we came; up Die Leer to the fringe of the plateau where I left my car and then to Bosluiskloof where at Seweweekspoort I knew of a farm with a telephone.

"I wanted to phone the hospital and warn the matron and staff.

"I planned to travel a few miles further to ask Louis la Grange of the farm Koueveld (Cold Field) to lend us his bakkie as an 'ambulance'.

"I certainly did not expect the chilly reception I got on my arrival.

"Doctor, we worried about you all night long! We even phoned the hospital to report that your car was deserted! Then we had to learn that you spent the night with a sister!

"From there on things went well.

"If ever a patient in the Ladismith hospital received tender loving care and was treated like a VIP, it was Sankie Marais. The staff did not leave her bedside for one minute and as far as possible they surrounded her with quiet and calm.

"Tetanus anti-toxin is very expensive, but we spared no cost and she got the best of everything. For several days she received huge doses. Fortunately, there was something like penicillin to which the tetanus bacillus is sensitive.

"She recovered completely. Before she returned she asked: 'How much do I owe you, Doctor?' I realised it was a matter of pride although money was never at issue.

"'Twenty pounds!' I said.

"Only in later years did I come to realise what a huge disservice I had done the Ladismith hospital by not publishing this case in the medical journal. It was the first case of settled tetanus that survived in those years. Since then, with muscle relaxants and other new medicines, the picture has changed completely.

"But above all the dedicated nursing pulled the patient through.

"And," he concludes, "some years later Cordier, the horseman with angina, died following a coronary thrombosis."

A decade or so before the last Kloovers left, Dr Manie Coetzee of Prince Albert caused a sensation when he flew into the Kloof.

He could speak feelingly about the problems of landing a Tiger Moth in the valley.

The first time he was called out, Koot Cordier had been bitten by a donkey. It was a matter of life or death. The wound looked dreadful.

Manie was the only doctor at Prince Albert at the time, the Kloovers say, and was summoned by a messenger on foot.

Manie was an experienced and enthusiastic pilot. He sent instructions on how an emergency landing strip should be prepared above the river. This the Kloovers did as best they could.

His patient had to be taken out immediately, but would not hear of this. Particularly not in a flying machine.

The doctor reasoned with him. He would not listen. The doctor argued with him, but Karel wouldn't budge. Then he showed him the alternative, the biggest injection needle! Karel went and survived.

"But to land or take off on that 'runway' was something else," Manie always said. "It was difficult enough to land on the short 'airstrip' over a low hillock, but one had to get out of the place too. Alive!

"Actually you don't land or take off. You arrive and depart. The usual procedures simply did not work in Gamkaskloof. You really had to rev the engine to depart."

In time Manie invented his own technique.

To "arrive" the plane engine must be cut as soon as the wheels touch down. Then the only alternative is to land because the engine could not be started from inside the plane. With the wheels on the ground, wings skirting the shrubs, the Moth runs in order to lose speed. It has no brakes. At the last moment the pilot jumps out and grabs the plane by the tail to stop it from falling into the sloot ahead.

Piet, Magriet and Fanie Swanepoel with doctor Manie Coetzee's Tiger Moth. (Photograph:*Nongqai*)

113

When "departing", he placed large stones in front of the wheels, started the engine and then tested it. Then he replaced the large stones with smaller ones to stop the vibrating plane from moving. He then jumped in, put all systems on "go" so that the plane could "jump" over the small stones. At the end of the "runway", the river runs in a low precipice, there he started to climb.

On another occasion a man — they think Koot Cordier — was in great pain and had to be flown out. Manie flew from Prince Albert to Gamkaskloof, picked up the patient and went on to George.

It was a cloudy and overcast day and they could not land immediately. He circled and circled until he saw an opening in the clouds. "The doctor immediately dropped through the hole," the story goes, "and then landed. The ambulance was waiting. Manie, who limps, was almost put on the stretcher, but he quickly pointed out the patient. When they arrived to carry him, he jumped up and assured them he was fine.

"He said he had a hernia but the whole thing jumped back when the plane 'fell down'".

After-the-road Kloovers counted it as one of the great blessings that an ambulance could get in and out.

But strangely no-one recalls anything unusual about such cases.

Chapter eight
Love and heartache

No-one knows of any wedding that took place in the Kloof. But everyone was properly "churched" in an outside ceremony.

Detailed genealogical charts have been drawn up by scholars about intermarriages. Of a total of eleven, seven per cent were inter-marriages and 35,25 per cent of the total were plural marriages. Several cases occurred of two brothers marrying two sisters.

There is no record of homosexuality.

The Kloovers had their own way of doing things. The big day in the life of a young couple was mostly an unforgettable festival. But before this there was much to be accounted for.

As soon as a young man started making eyes at the girls, he found the Kloof "different".

If he was an *inkommer*, he had to spell out in detail where he came from, who his forebearers were and from which "Jouberts/Olwages or whoever" he descended. Such an Inkommer caused problems for the girl. She was seriously cautioned by her folks. It was a recipe for clashes, because many daughters wanted to marry and get out.

In 1965 there was a memorable case. A young man was engaged for seven — some say 14 — years to "Ant Kowie's sister". Then Fanie came from Johannesburg to visit Kloof family and the sister left with the visitor.

Hannes Marais was an indigenous bachelor and at 59 still "waiting for the right girl to come along."

Sometimes daughters married against their parents' wishes. And left. These were seen as family tragedies.

"Piet and Ida were both Kloovers and were betrothed. Ida had already drawn the picture of her house and Piet started building. Then a young Botes fellow arrived on the scene and he and Ida left together never to return.

"Her parents sometimes heard from her, but Ida to this day, does not want to hear that she was born and bred in Gamkaskloof," the story goes.

One tale which is kept alive in the telling happened in the home of a well-known family.

The daughter went out to high school and lost her heart to a classmate.

When he was old enough, he went in to introduce himself to her family and discuss his intentions to court Dora and later marry her.

"The family was hospitable but when he left, hard and bitter words were exchanged. Dora refused to give him up and they forbade her to see him.

"Then she became pregnant.

"In spite of wanting to do the honourable thing, the parents still refused a marriage and chased Dora out of the house and told them 'never to set foot in the door again.'

"Her father became ill. On his deathbed his family pleaded with him to make peace with his child. She was a lovely person and he had always loved her dearly. Above all she was happily married.

"The pleading was in vain. She was disobedient and had flaunted his authority! She had turned her back on her family!

"He died without setting eyes on her again.

"And then it started. The haunting. The first time was when his wife Hessie was in the kitchen kneading dough. From their bedroom she clearly heard his voice calling: 'Dora! Dora, *my kind, kom terug*! (Dora, my child, come back!)'

"'No,'" Hessie decided, 'it's impossible. I'm getting old and am hearing voices.'" She carried on kneading the dough.

"Then the grandchildren who were playing outside came rushing in. *'Ouma!* Where is *Oupa*? We heard *Oupa* calling aunt Dora!'"

And so it went on. To this day...

Before politics came to the Kloof, there was unity. After politics, separation.

Came voting day the first time. Eric Louw, later Minister of Foreign Affairs in the National Party government, was the region's candidate. The Kloovers walked out to vote. It was a happy exodus with everyone talking and joking and guessing about the voting.

At the polling booths they were taken aside, treated like VIPs and thoroughly indoctrinated.

When they returned there were two groups. Enemies. The Nationalist supporters, wearing a yellow flower in their lapel, had won. The others — the SAPs — were "losers".

From that day on a Nat youngster who wanted to court a SAP's daughter, or vice versa, was out!

A legendary Kloof marriage was that of Ou Lewies Nel and his wife Katrien.

"Katrien was different!" Gamkaskloovers say. "She was young and Ou Lewies much older. "*Sommer nog* (still) a young girl when the "ou" married her."

Theo Olwage, a teacher in the Kloof, one day asked Lewies why he chewed tobacco and did not smoke a pipe like other Kloovers.

117

He said Katrien did not like it. So he stopped and took snuff. This she did not like either. Then he started chewing tobacco. She also didn't like that but he taught her to like it and she acquired the habit.

"One never saw Katrien actually chewing her cud, but she always had a *prop* (cud) in her cheek."

How Lewies found Katrien is a story in itself.

"Where you exit the Kloof near one of the drifts," the story goes, "Katrien's father lived.

"He was a hard man. Very hard! And very hard on Katrien! His only daughter.

"If a goat or a sheep was missing, she had to stay out until all hours to find it. *Tier* (leopard) or no *tier* she went out *meisiekindalleen* (girl alone) in the dark to look for it. She dared not come home without the missing animal.

"One night a goat was missing. Maybe it was a sheep. Katrien was by then an adolescent. Courtable.

"That night she did not return.

"Next day her father started looking for her. He searched and searched. No Katrien!

"Eventually he heard she was in Gamkaskloof.

"He knocked on the door of the first house in the valley. It was closed. He knocked again and Ou Lewies Nel opened it.

"Her father had not yet opened his mouth, when Ou Lewies started telling him a few *kaalkop* (bald) truths. About how he treated her like a hireling! And how bad.

"'She's not going back to you. She's staying here and I'm going to make her my wife.'

"Katrien was sixteen.

"That is how she came to live in the Kloof and earned herself a place in Klooflore.

"There are those who say it was from pure *orig-heid* (meddlesomeness) that he married such a young girl, but there are others who believe he had saved her from slavery.

"That a girl who grew up like Katrien did have problems is understandable.

"But she had her pride.

"Sometimes she came into the Kloof with a message for someone from Lewies. She wore silk stockings and clean high-heeled shoes. No-one could figure out how she did it because there were long stretches of road where the horse had to be led. Until someone saw Katrien travelling barelegged and barefooted and 'dressing up' just before her destination."

Another remembers: "She was almost at the end of a pregnancy when she came 'from up there' to find something to eat 'below'. Shame! They had lovely pumpkins and vegetables and things but she did not know how to run a proper household. Sometimes there was absolutely nothing to eat in the house and she came to exchange things for food.

"But Katrien grew up and became wiser, that is how the story ends."

Totally different was the marriage of Johanna Cordier to Tobie Dyssel of Oudtshoorn. Almost nondescript in Kloof drama style.

Tobie worked in Oudtshoorn and before their children's marriage, the families got together and arranged the wedding. Koot had a *bakkie* (light truck). It was after the road.

"He did not drive. He was driven to the wedding and the whole family attended the ceremony in the *Moederkerk* (Mother Church) and thereafter they enjoyed an intimate reception at the bridegroom's family home."

Family ties in the Kloof were generally strong.

In a sociological study done by Dr Brian du Toit of the University of Florida, he outlines the social patterns. Generally relatives visited relatives.

The 26 families — 200 souls — were studied and their visiting habits charted.

With such a clear social pattern there were no great problems as to whom should be invited to a wedding or rather who should be left out. It was an accepted conclusion.

The week before a wedding was crazy in some households. Large tobacco or caustic soda tins were neatly painted and often decorated beforehand. *Droëkoekies* (biscuits) and ginger and coconut biscuits, were made. These were kept in the tins. Ginger beer and wheat beer were prepared, and fresh coffee beans roasted and ground. Honey tea was picked when they flowered in the mountain, put in a bag in the outside oven to roast until light brown in colour and then chopped up. Tea was boiled before guests arrived. The longer it "stewd" the better the flavour.

Lenie Marais was indispensable at weddings. She was one of the few non-family members who was always invited. She had the delicate task of icing small cakes and made the rainbow and sponge cakes called *slapkoeke*. The bride's mother made the milk-tarts and small jam turnovers.

Lenie did the wedding cake.

The home where the reception was held, was prepared a day earlier. The *voorkamer* (sitting room) was decorated with leaves and ferns. Flower arrangements often included gladioli which grew well in Gamkaskloof and arum lilies which were plentiful.

The bridal table was covered with a *kleedjie* (crocheted tablecloth). Chairs for the bridal couple were decorated with ivy and flowers. Sometimes the reception was held under a large tree.

Koot Cordier describes his own wedding. Short and sweet. From a bridegroom's perspective: "Well, you see we walk out. Stay over with someone to-night. Or in the hotel. Tomorrow at nine the *predi-kant* (minister) marries you. Thank goodness the women didn't have *tierlantyntjies* (frippery) like to-day.

"Now you must take to the road early because *donkernag* (late at night) you arrive at Elandspad. That's if you cross the mountain at Weltevrede or Klippiesvlei.

"Tonight you dance till dawn with those tired legs and sore feet.

"Such a wedding isn't 'over' quickly. Our family easily held a reception for eight days.

"There's *karrie* (beer). That's about the only drink we know, except if you buy *witklip* (moonshine) at old Hartman's place at Groenfontein for a shilling a bottle."

But that was Koot's version.

Mothers and daughters describe weddings differently.

"The young couple walks out the night before, taking their wedding clothes with them. The ceremony is *vroegdag* (early in the day) so that they can walk back for the reception.

"Wedding clothes are exchanged for walking ones. At a prearranged place they dress in wedding clothes again for the reception.

"On the day of a marriage the atmosphere in the Kloof is different. One feels it. Guests walk to the bride's house and the womenfolk lend a hand with last-minute tasks. Chairs and *bankies* (benches) for the parents and important guests are dusted and pushed into place.

"Towards *middeldag* (midday) excitement mounts as the couple is expected at any moment.

"They slip in at the 'changing venue'.

"As soon as they appear, the children's shrieks of delight echo from the mountainsides.

"Sometimes the family makes a floral arch carried by youthful family members. Flower petals are strewn and they are accompanied by admiring dancing and singing youngsters."

The master of ceremonies was usually the teacher. Hostesses were appointed and *tant* Miem Mostert and Lenie Marais were favourites. Lenie was a jovial person and the heart and soul of a gathering.

Piet Joubert, Klein Piet and Johaans Rheeder were concertina players and anyone with an instrument like a guitar or mouth organ joined in. Failing this, music came from a His Master's Voice gramophone.

No alcohol was served. *Karrie* or *witblits* lusters had to bring their own. They were recognisable by their breath. They smelt of peppermints! The threshing floor had been prepared weeks before for the dancing.

"Whoever had a *vastrap* (a kind of dance) or waltz in his body, danced, old with young, tall with short."

Weddings were mostly held on Fridays so that the dancing could go on until dawn on Saturday morning. Kloovers respected the Sabbath.

Voordansers (leading dancers) were *tant* Lientjie Lood and *oom* Johaans Rheeder for the *riel*, *vastrap* and *skotteljons* (reel, hop-dance and cotillion). Late at night or early morning tired children came to their mothers who had warm things ready and made them comfortable on the hay next to the dance floor.

When the first rays of the sun came over the mountain top, the guests returned home with happy hearts and sore feet.

That, anyway, was how one memorable wedding was held.

Chapter nine
Misses and Sirs

The history of teaching in the Kloof follows the same official pattern that most schooling does; inseparable from the church.

There is an impression that the Kloof had a private school before the official one, but it remains just that, an impression.

The first official school was started by the Nederduits Gereformeerde Kerk (Dutch Reformed Church) of the Laingsburg area of the Cape Provincial Department of Education in 1904.

Danie Gerber of Joubertina was the first "government teacher".

Piet Marais donated the land for a school and a teacher's house.

Danie was "thoroughly informed" of circumstances in his new post and the needs in the Valley. He had to determine his own priorities because there were "many needs of which the Kloovers were unaware".

There is a plausible theory that with the start of the school, the first commercial deals were made, namely the exchange of groceries for raisins.

Teachers were honoured people. They were learned. Danie also acted as postmaster, magistrate and "agent" as lawyers were called. And he was a preacher.

Because of his contact with the world outside, and the narrow ties with Kloof children, his social position was unique. Although an *inkommer*, he was seen as wise, and his advice heeded.

In 1928 a second school was started in the middle of the Kloof. Here too the teacher was a prototype.

Schoolmaster Gerber and his pupils.
(Photograph: Dirk Lilienfeld)

The two schools, one at Onderplaas and the other at Boplaas, could still be remembered before the end of the nineteenth century. Mr Oosthuizen is best remembered at Boplaas and Mr Bosman at Onderplaas.

The change in Kloof lifestyle was huge. Also for adults.

Marina Nortier (Ehlers) was the last teacher (1958/59) and it was part of her self-imposed duty to bring in books and magazines. "The general love of reading was amazing! There was a thirst for knowledge!" she recalls. All this brought about by earlier teachers.

The religious metamorphosis was the largest. Prayer meetings were held monthly and the school became the church during weekends. This was a binding factor in a diverse society.

A further "revolution" followed. People had to "dress" for church gatherings.

One can but imagine the attitude of the men of The Hell when their wedding suits came out of mothballs where they had been lying since that day; mostly short jackets just below the waist, buttoned to the neck with a white strip of collar showing.

The women took out hats from a forgotten era, decorated them with ribbons and bows and flowers.

Most Kloof women had long hair tied into a knot. To accommodate this coil they wore hats with high crowns.

Their creativity was satisfied in their dresses. The *lapgoed* (material) for the mother was black crêpe, the bodice decorated with tiny tucks. White or cream crocheted lace collars and cuffs were added.

Teenage daughters were dressed in puffed-sleeve blouses generously decorated with tiny tucks and lace insets. The skirt was floral Tobralco and the *uitskop onderrok* (bouffant) flared. Little girls also wore skirts and blouses but with long socks instead of stockings.

A prayer meeting started with the community singing spiritual songs. There was a *voorsanger* (lead singer); mostly a woman.

Meester (schoolmaster) conducted the service and was clad in a sober black suit. One such "master/ teacher/preacher" is indelibly etched in many Kloof memories. He read long chapters from the Dutch Bible. Then he preached about the sins of people and all their sinful inclinations. His own words distressed him so much that he had to sit down to recover from his weeping.

"Aunt Leentjie of the gentle disposition," they say, "always cried with him and had to use her handkerchief freely."

The rest were mostly uncomfortable, fidgeted in their seats, looked at the wall, inspected their hands and fingernails and waited until master regained his composure.

"And," they add "this was the self-same man who could be so damn silly with the girls."

"*Ons moes hom regsien*"! ("We had to put him in his place). The children followed a normal school curriculum and did well. They not only followed prescribed lessons, but learnt much more.

Gamkaskloof children.
(Photograph: Dirk Lilienfeld)

A very popular teacher brought in a love of gardening. He had a thorough knowledge of plants which he shared with the community. Flower gardens were made and when they saw how well bulbs like gladioli did in his garden, they wanted some as well. They learnt about shrubs and other beautiful plants that would do well in the Kloof.

The children were amazed to learn that the ordinary raisin-bush, for instance, was used by the Bushmen to make reed flutes, and their most important weapon, the bow.

The candle-bush, which every Kloover knew, got its name from the primitive folks who lit a green branch because it burnt so long.

The *spekboom* (*Portulacaria afra*) was the water tank in times of drought. The juice in the small fat leaves was highly esteemed by early man and beast.

There was the *botterboom* (*Cotyledon paniculata*) about which the children taught the teacher.

Karoo children always loved *botterboom* rides. More so in the Kloof because the terrain was so suitable.

The best ski-slope was at Vloer-se-Kloof. High up on the steep cliffs the rock surfaces were smoothed by water running over them for centuries. *Botterboom* was plentiful.

An aspiring skier cut a thick branch: the ski. He or she would then drag it to the top, put it in position and sit astride it. A slight push sets the skier in motion at a speed much faster than a *foefieslaaid* (type of rope slide) at a 45° angle.

It was no easy sport. In fact, it was forbidden by most parents because it was so dangerous. Arms, legs, backs and necks could be broken on this course which gained speed as it became more slippery with every ride. The *botterboom* had a soapy fluid which "oiled" the track.

Many a child was spanked soundly when the mother found tell-tale green marks on their clothes and they confessed to having been disobedient.

Whether or not the teacher was impressed with this information, is not known. But he did teach them to look after trees, particularly the Karee and thorn trees, the source of firewood and kraal walls. Conservation was part of everyday life.

Aloes which are plentiful, were highly rated for their medicinal value. The thick leaf was cut and its yellowish juice mixed with a bit of flour to make a pill. Two small bitter aloe pills were used as a laxative.

These same aloes often left a family without milk for days if the milch goat feasted on the flowers. Bitter as gall was the milk!

The children learnt about survival in the mountains. The succulent *ghaap* (*Trichocaulon piliferum*) could be chewed to suppress hunger and thirst. (What a dietary plant!)

The *kruidjie-roer-my-nie* (honey-flower) was known as a medicinal plant by the adults, but the children loved sucking out the flower's sweet syrup.

It was a teacher who introduced them to a washing machine. He brought one in and every man, woman and child went to look at how it was turned by hand and how clean it made the washing. It was, however, a psychological and social shock when he announced that in future not his wife, but he would do the washing.

The Kloof was blessed with many good teachers.

Marina Nortier is remembered fondly for the emancipation she brought in. She taught mothers and daughters the art of make-up. Soon after Marina's demonstration, lipstick and so on were on the Kloovers shopping list.

She was the first woman to wear slacks.

Were the Kloof mothers horrified? Not at all! Narrowmindedness was not the Kloovers' way.

But there was the teacher — her name long forgotten — who only stayed for 11 days. She lived with a Kloof family and announced one morning that she was going out to see a doctor. She borrowed a blanket, went up Die Leer never to be seen again.

The walls of the houses were built with raw clay-bricks which comprised a mixture of cow-dung or straw and stones. For the foundations, slate or shingles were used. (Photograph: Paul A. Coetzer)

Flat roofs were constructed from thick wooden poles with a layer of reeds on top. They were bolted up with the bark of thorn-trees. On top of that came a lyer of mud and clay. The salt in the clay cristallised and prevented the roofs from leaking. (Photograph: Paul A. Coetzer)

The exit to Prins Albert from Bopoort. The Gamka River flows through it. (Photograph: Paul A. Coetzer)

The house of Mr Piet Mostert. (Photograph: Paul A. Coetzer)

The blanket was greatly missed.

That school term the children had vacation.

Johannes and Enone Theron feature in several Kloof stories.

They came from Postmasburg, turned off, visited the valley and the breathtaking natural beauty of the place decided them when Johannes was offered the vacant post as schoolmaster.

They were not very happy. Enone apparently often admitted that "a woman had to love her husband dearly to follow him to the Kloof." She missed a social life and more company.

She did, however, praise the women of Gamkaskloof for not gossiping. "Badmouthing" she said, "and harmful stories do not exist."

To this day, Enone is remembered as the person who approached the Carnegie Foundation to test the children psychologically and intellectually. She and Johannes were worried about the children's ability to adapt to outside schools as the result of possible intermarriages. "Their lives and horizons like the geography ended on the mountain tops and stimulation from outside was practically non-existent," they thought.

The Foundation found the IQ of Kloof children to be higher than the average of children in schools of surrounding towns. They found the stimulation of natural surroundings and unspoilt nature played a big role. The Therons are remembered for other incidents.

"You see," they'll say, "things were not easy for teachers. *Riempies* had to be cut very thin. (They were poor.) Small salaries. But a little car was a MUST. Bought on tick."

Gamkaskloovers were not exactly poverty-stricken in spite of their simple life-styles. The table overflowed with everything that was needed. "But there was not much money," they said.

"Enone had a little Volkswagen Beetle. Her own. She came from the Kalahari and knew about night-hunting.

"So Johannes drives. Marita sits next to him. Enone and Hendrik sit in front. In the boot. They take out one of the headlights. Enone shines it in the veld. From the front. In the boot. The car travels with one headlight. Hendrik is a good shot. With a pistol. They see two bright eyes and he shoots right between them. Now they have some meat for the table."

Johannes and Enone made the best of their stay. They were hospitable and received friends.

Once three strangers spent three months with them. They were so intrigued with Gamkaskloof that they could not leave.

Synonymous with Middelplaas School were the Marais family. Sankie (who recovered from tetanus) and Lenie Marais were sisters. Sankie came in as teacher in the 1920s, married a farmer and became a permanent Kloover.

Single teachers often boarded with them. Couples had a house near Sankie's.

Martiens Snyman was chairman of the Parent/ Teachers Association and was respected as such.

Lenie and Willem Marais were part of the "school clan" as their house was close by and children like the Nels who lived seven miles further, boarded with them during the week.

For the children this was sheer joy. No atmosphere of a school hostel in the home of the bubbling, fun-loving, and energetic *tant* Lenie. They helped with domestic chores much as they would normally do in their own homes because *"ledigheid is die duiwel se oorkussing,"* (idleness is the devil's bolster) Lenie said.

The school was the information centre of the Kloof. All notices, church and government ones, were sent to the school and the news was spread by the children.

In 1953 Gamkaskloof became a separate area of the NG Kerk (Dutch Reformed Church) with their own *ouderling* (elder) and *diaken* (deacon). It was, however, difficult for these *kerkraadslede* (church council members) to attend meetings in Prince Albert.

The preachers visited the congregations periodically, held services and baptised children.

The last child to be baptised was Pieter Gerhardus (Pierre) Mostert. He was born in Prince Albert on 7 June 1979 "when his mother Dorothea Caroline and his father Pieter Gerhardus were *horingoud* (as old as the hills). In 1986 he went out to school followed by his parents. Many a minister, even after the road, was happy to negotiate the Kloof on horse back as "the road was hard on cars".

Ds Du Toit of Prince Albert and his elder, however, recalls a hearty reception in the homes of Johaans Mostert and the teachers Bosman and Oosthuizen where they "were given separate bedrooms".

Children who were not christened in the Kloof were taken to the parsonage when it was convenient.

Once there was a severe rift in the normal steady pace of the religious folk when a so-called sect arrived.

Strong differences about religious beliefs and rites surfaced and — something unheard of — criticism was levelled at the NG Kerk.

In 1949 the Afrika Evangelie Bond (Africa Gospel Union) came in and held services and prayer meetings.

Ministers in Prince Albert first heard about it in a note from Mynie Mostert who was unhappy because "Mrs Marais, the teacher, refused them the school premises".

Mrs Marais also wrote, without mincing her words, how people followed the young evangelists like "hungry vultures". She refused to open the school because "parents take their children with them at night and the following day they are good for nothing in school." She added: "The Kloovers blame the NG Kerk because we do not have a minister or a church. The ministers at Prince Albert do not even know our people."

This letter must have shaken up the church council. An additional minister was appointed and the Kloovers were informed that "things would improve in future".

Time ran out for the Gamkaskloof school after the road. Parents could, and did, convey their children to surrounding towns. The children fitted in with the larger groups and many of them simply disappeared in the outside world.

In 1959, three years before the "aorta to the heart outside" was built, the last school at Middelplaas was waning. There were 23 families, 130 souls and only 13 children in the school. The Boplaas school had been in disuse for some years. Today, the shells are still there along with the ghost houses in which only memories of the Kloof in its heyday of seclusion, remains.

Chapter ten
Unforgettables

Kloovers have mixed sentiments about their past life. There is appreciation. But it was a hard life.

Yet in every story there is some unforgettable pleasantry.

Like the Sunday midday meal.

Generally, the main meal was at night, but Sundays were different. It was a day of rest for man and beast. The mother spoilt her family with a generous pot-roast and small potatoes browned in the gravy. Sweet potatoes were layered with thin slices of unpeeled orange, with a crumbed ginger biscuit topping. Spanspek, sweet as honey, or an even sweeter watermelon was dessert.

When seats around the dining-room table ran out, the children sat on cushioned wall seats round the room.

There were memorable times when the orchards or mealie and wheat fields had to be guarded against feasting birds and baboons.

Unforgettable were the days when the children took their father's lunch to the field. Fresh bread warm from the oven, cut in *skaapwagtersnye* (very thick slices) and plastered with home-made butter and a few squares of honey with a can of buttermilk with butter crumbs on top.

There were spooky things like centipedes and *dikdaaie* as the *bloukopkoggelmander* (blue-headed lizard) was called. Sometimes the children teased the *klipgeitjie* (stone gecko) until it dropped the end of its tail scuttling away safely with the tail piece wriggling on the stone.

Water snakes were abundant in rivers and streams and while the Kloof child caught tadpoles, eels or crabs, they watched snakes catching frogs. Herding goats and sheep on the mountain slopes evoked many rich and vivid memories.

And stories.

"A ewe goat bleated loudly every afternoon at a certain time.

"Then stopped as suddenly as it had started.

"Everytime the herder was just too late to find which goat was so distressed.

"Naturally, there was no shortage of theories and scary stories.

"Could it be a *tier* (leopard)? No! He would have caught her.

"Baboons? No! They don't catch ewes, only lambs.

"The truth eventually silenced even the most imaginative theoretician.

"A goatherd saw it 'with his own two eyes' one afternoon. There was a large snake hanging from the ewe's teat. 'Like a snake swallows a mouse, he swallowed the teat. In his mouth!' he reported. And during the sucking the ewe was peaceful."

But why then was she bleating?

Maybe to call the snake. Maybe her udder was uncomfortably full.

Who knows.

This could not be tolerated and the ewe was placed in a different grazing area. Her milk production returned to normal.

A similar incident occurred a couple of years later.

Karel Cordier says he and his ten brothers and sisters regularly drank milk from a goat's teat when herding them.

They also loved to hunt; wild ducks, small rhebuck

and *klipbokke*. In the winter months kudu was hunted for biltong.

Donkey rides were fun. Very few boys could resist them and a few tomboyish girls joined in. One donkey is separated from the herd and a rope tied round its neck. The rider gets on, someone "slap starts" him and if the donkey rider is lucky, he or she remains on top for a few paces before ploughing head first into the kraal manure.

Or the donkey jibs and kicks his hindlegs in the air when mounted with the prospective rider flying forward through the air. Nosediving into the kraal manure.

Hunting for beehives was something children did naturally. When gadding about in the mountains, they always kept an eye open for bees.

Karel Cordier was known as *Karel Ratel* (honey badger) because he feared not even the worst bee stings when gathering honey.

Unforgettable because of his place in Kloof memories, is a certain Rheeder who, in the *voorjare* (early years) lived on Gamka heights when he spotted a honey thief near a marked hive.

"He sat in the shade of his house one hot summer afternoon keeping an eye on the goats against the opposite krantz, when he saw someone at one of his hives. Openly. Right opposite his house!

"Such things were not tolerated. Rheeder fetched his .303 and took up position. His wife came outside. She wanted to know what he wanted with a gun. He told her and she was terribly upset. 'Look first! It might be a Kloover!' But he would not listen.

"He took aim and shot. And a man fell down the krantz.

"His wife begged him to go and look, but he refused. He would go when it suited him! When next he went to Calitzdorp! He would most certainly not go and climb around the mountain for a thief! A honey thief at that!

"Three months later he had to go to Calitzdorp.

"At Matjiesvlei he met a man looking for work. Rheeder needed workers. They were busy harvesting beans.

"The man wanted to know where the farm was. Rheeder explained *vers en kapittel* (chapter and verse) and added: 'It's in Gamkaskloof.'"

The story goes: "That brown man turned grey! 'Gamkaskloof!' he shouted. 'No! Never in Gamkaskloof! Never!'

"He lifted the hat from his head.

"He revealed a wide cut and told Rheeder how one day not so long ago he quite innocently went to cut a bee hive in Gamkaskloof when a bullet cut 'this parting on my skull'."

Stealing fruit was not a general *kwaaijongstreek* (mischievous youth prank), probably because all Kloovers had an abundance of everything on their own farms.

Yet a spanspek-loving Cordier once long ago could not wait for his own crop to ripen and coveted his brother's early crop. He put his feet in two weaver bird nests to cover his tracks and for a few nights feasted to his heart's content.

"His brother noticed the theft and, of course, knew immediately the thief was not a baboon!

"He set a trap and…" on that note the story ends.

Koot Cordier's name pops up in most Kloof stories. Often not as a story on its own. They are "by-the-way" ones.

"Even though Koot told the shop assistant how the *tier* caught one of his many children the other night, no person was ever attacked by an animal or killed."

Whether Koot with this story of his family's dreadfully dangerous and primitive living circumstances so touched the poor girl's heart that she added extra sweets and things for the survivors, one has to find out for oneself.

Telephones came to Gamkaskloof before the road. The Swanepoels were the first to have one.

Koot's daughter worked in Oudtshoorn and was arranging her wedding. She left a message that her father be at the telephone at a given time, as she wanted to discuss something with him.

It was the first time Koot saw "the thing".

"The phone rings. Magriet Swanepoel says Koot should pick up and answer. It's his call.

"He picks it up and his daughter speaks. *'Is dit jy, Pa?'* (Is that you, Dad?)

"But Koot throws the instrument down shouting: *'Die blêrrie ding praat dan met my!'"* (The bloody thing is talking to me!)

Another unforgettable Koot Cordier story is about a man who came to buy a goat.

"Now the goats are grazing on the opposite mountain slopes. Koot sits at home. Below.

"'Now which goat do you want?' he asks.

"The man points one out. With a red head.

"Koot goes into the house and brings out his .303. He takes aim, shoots the animal in his stride and tells the buyer to go and fetch it himself.

"Only much later does it come out it was not even one of Koot's goats."

Kloof children grew up with the same respect for wildlife as their parents had. They hunted for the pot. And eradicated vermin like lynx and jackal. There was and still is, considerable wild life in the Swartberg Mountain including lynx, jackal, werewolves, wild dogs, otters, mongoose, polecats and leopards.

Once the Marais brothers suffered a great loss when 20 of their goats disappeared.

Their shooting skills were well known. "They could set a gun pointing to a trap which kills with one shot," Kloovers remember.

Word was spread that a gun trap was put up. Everyone was on guard. They slept fitfully at night waiting for the gun to go off.

When it happened, they found "a strange animal like nothing they'd ever seen before. A cross between a wild dog, a wolf and something else." Then the thieving stopped.

When interesting characters in the Kloof are discussed one or other Cordier features somewhere.

"Piet Cordier was a *duiwel met 'n geweer* (a devil with a gun) you'll hear. Target shooting and bisleys were favourite sports with Kloof men. Often the prize was a cake, but sometimes a sheep or a goat.

"Karel Cordier was a crack marksman and shot himself into Klooflore unforgettably as a young man when he and his prospective father-in-law went hunting. He missed the first buck but pulled down the following three in the running.

"The story started when Karel went to ask for permission to marry (*ouersvra*). No-one could keep up with him when walking. Or dancing. 'But can you shoot?' *oom* Awie Marais asked.

"They left with a can of *karrie*. At the river he shot some rock pigeons in their flight. Then the three buck.

"Karel was as much of a *platjie* (imp) as his *oupa* Koot.

"Once a donkey bit him. Dr Manie Coetzee flew him out to hospital in his plane.

"At the hospital they asked him how old he was and he replied that he had to walk out of The Hell to register his birth."

Many outsiders wanted to believe that the Kloovers were primitive and bred like rabbits. Particularly those of neighbouring towns.

Such stories were topics of interest to tourists and visitors. So Koot Cordier played along when a shop-keeper asked him: "How many children do you have?"

"Wife!" he asked. "How many do we have now? And don't count the three that were caught by the *tiers*."

He told the headmaster at Prince Albert High School when he registered his eldest, that he had three-and-a-half dozen children. And he was not lying. It was a typical Kloof riddle. He had nine children.

Piet Cordier was not only a crack marksman but his strength was legendary.

"He carried his wife's Dover cast-iron stove… and carried it on his shoulders from Prince Albert… right into her kitchen. And… when he bought the stove he paid with a handful of gold coins."

Money stories are part of Kloof tales. No-one talks about their own affairs. It is always someone else's.

The fact is, Kloovers did not think much of money. As long as they kept a good table and could afford necessities, the rest was put into *trommels* (trunks) under their bed.

"In 1930, South Africa went off the gold standard." So starts one story.

"And a few *stinkryk* (stinking rich) Cordiers, were buried with their fortunes intact.

"Koot Cordier was buried in front of Grootkloof. His house was nearby.

"He made his fortune from *witblits*," the apocryphal story goes.

One after-the-road story tells how police "absolutely ruined" a good *dagga* (marijuana) field "and took the wealthy farmer away."

During his last years, Koot Cordier apparently always sat in a certain place watching a beehive. If anyone asked what he was watching, he would answer: "That no-one tampers with my bees." But everyone knew Koot kept a trunk filled with gold pounds under the hive.

And there is the true story of Piet Cordier who was visited by "a man from the government" who said he was sent to buy up all gold pounds because it would lose its value after the gold standard changeover. The bighearted official offered five shillings for every pound. "You see," he explained, "the pounds will have to be handed in later anyway and will be worth nothing."

Piet took out his *velsak* (buckskin) full of gold pounds and emptied it. It was carefully counted and he received his full quote of crowns as five shilling pieces were called. And a receipt!

"And" the story goes "no-one ever found out who this swindler was and where he went."

Another Kloof character who is still vividly remembered is *Bont Sanna* (Mottled Sanna). And particularly by the Mostert clan. A gold pound is involved.

"You see," the story begins, "the Esterhuizes were fair-skinned coloured folk. During the Spanish flu in 1918 they all died. Their graves are in the Kloof with their names scratched on 'headstones'. Some nights when you pass there, your hair stand on end and you know this is the Esterhuizes graveyard.

"Sanna was a redhead and freckled. So she was called Bont Sanna. She was "also a bit slow in the head." She rode an ostrich. Her choice of transport.

"Her folks regularly sent her on errands and with notes. Sometimes *doodsbriefies* (death notices) when someone had died. From Bokloof to Onderkloof she stopped at every house. Sanna carried the letter in a little box tied under her *kappie* (bonnet).

"She sat on her ostrich hen.

"You see, her grandfather farmed with ostriches but her grandmother said if ostrich meat were ever cooked in one of her pots, she would never use it again." In the manner of most Kloof stories many minor tales are woven into the main story.

"Her father inherited the ostriches and the birds multiplied.

"They became wild and ou Lekkerjan hunted them. He told everyone if you wanted to shoot an ostrich on the run, you aimed just behind him when he lifted his leg. You kept that height in the eye and when you fired, his head went flying."

"Well then! Bont Sanna rode all over the place and children did not leave her alone.

"One day she brought the farm rent to *oupa* Henk Mostert. The gold pound in the little box under her *kappie*. The Mostert children teased her. Sanna's *kappie* fell on the ground and one of them picked it up and cemented it into the bedroom wall which was being built.

"Only much later the story of the pound in the *kappie* came to light, but by then the wall was dry and completed.

"And that gold pound is in the Mostert house to this day."

Klein Koot Cordier's Joseph Rogers pen-knife became the property of Henk Mostert through Sanna and her ostrich.

A Joseph Rogers was a much-desired object.

"Sanna arrived when the two were deep in conversation. The ostrich saw the shiny blade of the open knife and swallowed it. Kleinkoot was terribly upset. He tried to throttle the bird to get his knife back. *Oupa* Henk stopped him. 'You'll kill the bird! The knife is open!'"

Kleinkoot left *boos-boos*! (very cross). Then *oupa* Henk calmly shut the knife in her throat, put his hand down her neck and took it out, saying: "*Weg-gooigoed is hougoed* (finding's keepings).'"

It wasn't only coins and knives that disappeared. Once it was a farm. If there's any truth to the story.

The fireside tale relates how a Cordier sold Boplaas to Gustaf Nefdt. Nefdt rented the farm to "ou Piet Botes". The Cordier sons moved to the eastern Kloof. Years later Nefdt sold the farm to Japie Calitz.

Only then did the story surface of how the credulous Cordier went to Prince Albert with the prospective buyer. Some believe it was to Calitzdorp. There Cordier was taken to Die Oog (a pub) and "treated royally". The documents of sale were signed then and there "and" the story concludes, "when he sobered up all he had left were the clothes on his body."

Another story concerns the time a television crew filmed at Gamkaskloof.

"Annie Basson made the programme *Van Gister en Eergister* (Of Yesterday and the Day Before) and extras were needed at R34 a day!

"So, along comes Koot Cordier. Before he moves he insists on a *jangroentjie* (peppermint liqueur). After all it is a very important occasion!

"Now Koot's *ewemens* (alter ego) is Jan-Frans. He walks like Koot. If Koot *slingers* (staggers) Jan-Frans *slingers*. Koot has an ulcer. Jan-Frans has an ulcer. When Koot doubles up with pain so does Jan-Frans."

This story you find out is not about Koot but about Jan-Frans and it leads to one about Jan Bloubos (Jan Blue Bush).

"He was unforgettable. Children were not allowed to address him by name. Only respectfully as Outa Bloubos.

"Now you see, Jan Bloubos came in with Anna Meintjies' team of aloe cutters. He stayed on. To help

Stefaans Swanepoel with his wheat crop. Next to the Gamka River.

"Jan Bloubos never slept in a house or a room. Long ago he had heard about the *tokkelossie* (gremlin). And he was scared! Very scared! Not just very scared! Terrified! Every night he built a huge fire and crept under the *bloubos* (Diospyros) to sleep.

"He and Stefaans Swanepoel grew up together," someone adds. "He came in when he was an *opgeskote klong* (adolescent youth).

"There under the *bloubos* he kept cups and saucers for his Kloof visitors. And he made delicious coffee for them. Hospitable he was indeed.

"Once he went to visit Koot Cordier's workers across the Gamka River. The water level had risen over the weekend and on Monday morning he could not return.

"A few days later the water subsided.

"Jan Bloubos did not cross. He would not give a reason. Everyone knew it was because *tokkelossie* lives in the water.

"He said to Koot Cordier: 'Ja! Today Stefaans Swanepoel will say Jan Bloubos will stay on the other side till the crabs walk on dry sand before he crosses!'

"The Swanepoels cared for Jan for many years. Then he took ill. It was serious and they took him to Cape Town for treatment. There he died but they brought his body back and buried him in Calitzdorp."

Another Swanepoel's — Piet's — two cart-horses feature in a story. Or maybe it is Martiens Snyman's story.

It might upset animal lovers. But it was part of Kloof reality.

"Martiens had a gift with animals. Few people are so blessed.

"Piet Swanepoel had two beautiful, black cart-horses. Cars they would pull, but balked at a plough. Piet could not get them to move a hoof when he needed to plough his fields.

"One day Piet battled for half-an-hour with the obstinate animals while Martiens sat on his stoep watching.

"He crossed the stream to Piet's field."

Koos van Zyl, the road-builder, was working on the inside Kloof road and saw it all. He was so intrigued that he switched off his bulldozer to see what would happen. He takes up the story.

"Martiens talks. Piet talks. One horse actually lies down, it is so obstinate.

"Then Martiens tells Piet to fetch dry *kraalbossies* and put them next to the horse. Martiens takes out his matches and lights the *bossies*. When the flames are higher than the horse's back, he gets up.

"Martiens talks to him. Whispers. Softly. Gently. And... there they go with the plough. Martiens ploughed two furrows and handed them back to Piet with the words: 'Now carry on!'

"Kleinkoot Cordier and his *oupa* Koot always played a game of hiding a pin. One afternoon Kleinkoot came to *Oupa* to get *witklip* but first they played 'hide the pin'.

"Earlier Kleinkoot had provoked *Oupa* by accusing him of selling him *voorloop* or *naloop*; inferior *witblits*.

"Then Kleinkoot hid the pin. *Oupa* searched but could not find it. The rest of the family eventually helped him but nobody could find the pin.

"Tradition is tradition and what he could not solve himself remained unsolved. Even if it drove the person crazy.

"Kleinkoot enjoyed his victory enormously. So much so, that he laughed with a wide open mouth.

144

Oupa was so vexed he picked up a handful of sand and threw it 'right down Kleinkoot's throat'."

Two outsiders who feature in many Kloof tales are Piet Botha, the stock inspector, and Theuns Coetzee, the police officer.

Botha is said to have given the name Die Hel (The Hell) to Gamkaskloof; a name which outsiders use but Kloovers dislike. So much so, that a journalist who asked directions to The Hell at a farm in the Swartberg Mountains was told: "The Hell? No, mister! We in the mountains have our little sins and so on, but you won't find Hell in the Little Karoo."

Botha was also an excellent stone thrower and could kill a bird or chicken on the run.

Piet Cordier and Piet Botha "always had something going". They regularly tried to outwit each other. With pranks.

"One day Botha came softly down Die Leer. Cordier was irrigating his fields. Today I'll '*trek*' him a '*streep*' (play a trick), thought Botha.

"When he was close enough, he fired a shot just above Cordier's head, to frighten him. Cordier shot back and hid behind a rock.

"He called his son and they pinpointed the 'attacker's' position. They fired alternately and kept Botha where he was.

"Eventually Botha held out his hat. They shot his hat full of holes." And the end of the story: "That day Botha had to work in the hot sun without a hat and had blisters on his *bles* (bald patch)."

Botha was not always the loser. One day he turned the tables on Cordier.

Again Cordier was irrigating his mealie lands. Or maybe the vegetable patch. Botha arrived unseen. Cordier went further and further into the orchard under the trees. It was dense.

"Botha climbed into a tall pear tree, found his seat,

then called out in a hollow graveyard voice: 'Piet!' And again: 'Piet!'

"Cordier looked around but saw no-one and could not puzzle out what was going on. He carried on watering.

"Again the voice from above rang out: 'Piet! Piet!' He looked around then it dawned on him that the voice was not from the earth. It was from above him. He was visibly shaken.

"When the pulpit voice called for the third time, Cordier threw the spade down, took off his hat and held it over his heart and said: *'Spreek, Here! U dienskneg luister!'* (Speak, Lord! Thy servant is listening!)"

Theuns Coetzee once had to attend to a police task in the Kloof and he met up with Botha.

Botha normally shouted from the top of Die Leer announcing his arrival to Cordier. This day they came down quietly and planned a prank. They talked it over thoroughly. Botha would fire a shot just above Cordier's head and at that instant Coetzee would throw a mud clot against his back.

"Cordier was deep in thought. Absent. Far away in mind and spirit.

"They stole up on him. Coetzee gave the sign. He was ready.

"When the shot rang out and the clot struck, Cordier fell flat on his back, boots in the air. 'I've been shot!' he yelled. 'I've been shot!'

"When the two *boosdoeners* (evil-doers) appeared in stitches and helpless with laughter at the sight of Cordier, he got up and swore he would get back at them."

Relations with the police were not always cordial. The officers had their work to do. And fact was that even when the hunting season was closed, a Kloover's gunbarrel was always open.

After Piet Cordier's earlier *onderonsie* (altercation) with the law about *witblits* sales, one can only guess that the humiliated constable had "his knife in" for Piet.

Law is law and the Kloovers should never get the idea that they are above the law.

Zannie van der Walt who knows The Hell through and through readily admits that ten per cent of the stories are true. Many of the rest are "salted, peppered and spiced".

So the story goes that one day the *konstabeltjie* (constable) put his hand on Piet's shoulder while he was busy — outside the hunting season — cutting off the head of a ribbok.

"'I've been after you for a long time!' he said triumphantly. 'Now I've got you!'

"Piet was philosophical. 'Ja, Konstawel! That's life for you. Today you win. Tomorrow I win.'

"The constable took the buck's head and put it in his saddlebag and left with the evidence.

"That's when Piet flew into action. His family! Someone must help him urgently! It's a court case!

"He remembered that someone's donkey had foaled the previous day.

"Piet ordered: 'Cut off the head! Now!'

"They argued and talked and talked and argued. 'Piet you're asking too much. A donkey!' (Remember that his donkey was to an early Kloover what a bakkie was after the road).

"But family is family. And the honour of a member was in jeopardy.

"Then Piet ordered: 'Quickly! Follow him! Immediately! Yes you! And you! Not me! He doesn't know you. He'll spend the night at Weltevrede if I'm right.'"

"Kloovers were fast walkers. Much quicker than outsiders. They caught up with the constable and spent the night at Weltevrede.

"The next morning a proud police officer arrived at Prince Albert police station.

"'At last I've got Piet Cordier where I want him! Here is the evidence!' Triumphantly he opened his saddlebag and the donkey foal's head dropped out!

"You see," the story goes, "Piet did say: 'Today you win! Tomorrow I win'."

Once, long ago, Piet Botha agreed to accompany two reporters of the now defunct *Brandwag* magazine into The Hell. Beforehand they were told in Prince Albert that "everyone has a still and they drink *witblits* like others drink tea and coffee."

And warned: "In heaven's name, don't stay overnight. You never know what can happen! Strangers are shot at for na reason. All that remains of you will end up in a hole with your name on it."

With these impressions in mind the impish Piet Botha took the two fellows, a journalist and a photographer, to Die Leer. From the top he saw Piet Cordier in his fields. He took his gun and fired a shot about ten yards above Cordier's head.

Cordier shouted to his son: "*Bring my lat!*" (Fetch my rifle!) Then shots rang out. The journalist did not record their reaction.

Eventually Botha shouted: "Hey! Don't shoot! It's Piet Botha!"

Cordier showed himself and pointed threateningly at Die Leer. "And," the journalist takes up the incident, "there he comes with buoyant strides, briskly like a man half his age and in the prime of life, up Die Leer with ease. He meets us and helps carry our equipment while we battle on with aching legs and painful knees."

Krisjan Cordier brought a group of journalists down Die Leer. He chatted away merrily while the stressed men were clawing their way down expecting to fall to their death at any moment. Krisjan told them how easily donkeys negotiated Die Leer. Particularly the one with the *pêreloog* (cataract) which he [Krisjan] eventually cured with finely grounded centipedes.

"You should try it sometime," he advised.

He was obviously proud of the Valley and the Cordier lands. "A bucketful of this soil in Boplaas is worth more than a whole countryful outside!"

He pointed at an orange tree. "That's where we always buried dogs which had *vrekked* (died). You can see this tree is thirty feet tall." He picked an orange and tastes it. "Sweeter than sugar!

"This," he says, "is where you hear dogs bark any time of the day or night when there's not a dog in sight."

This writer, as a journalist, once had the fun of writing a headline: "Five Dutch Reformed Church ministers head straight to Hell," when I learnt of the intended trip.

Another unforgettable character was Lenie Marais.

She pops up in many Kloof stories but they are contradictory, obviously, "well-salted, peppered and highly spiced". Perhaps because she was so different from the average Kloover, she set the imaginations racing. Lenie died in her nineties.

Her brother Mias Pretorius in "injury time" moved from Calitzdorp to a family member in Lichtenburg. He tells how the family arrived in Gamkaskloof.

"The Pretorius children grew up in Matjiesvlei. Sankie went to teach in the Kloof and married Andreas Marais and settled there.

"Then in December 1921 there was an enormous flood. Everything on Father's grounds were washed away. Everything! Animals! Everything!

"Sankie and Andreas invited the whole family to move in with them.

"We took a few bare necessities as we had no intention of staying on.

"Then Andreas offered Father a piece of land on which to farm. We lived with them while Father built our house. That is the house in which Lenie and her husband Willem Marais lived after their marriage.

"In later years Lenie made changes to the house. I'm sad to say that she was far more diligent than he was. She was hard-working. A sort of *mannetjies-mens* (amazon). She farmed and worked like a man. Always busy."

To *Brandwag* journalists who visited her in the 1940s she said: "Nowadays I feel at home in my house. It used to have one bedroom. I hired a builder to enlarge it but he was so slow that I chased him away and did the work myself. The fireplace I built. And the chimney. They said a woman could not build a fireplace. Mine works fine. I got it right the first time!"

Lenie and Willem's house is the only gabled building in the Kloof. The windows are decorated with white pebbles. This she did herself. In the *voorkamer* there is a slasto dado. Earlier she decorated it with sea shells which were allegedly picked up at Sea Point, but during the restoration — it is not clear when — they were damaged and removed and the dado added.

There are many stories in circulation about this Marais house. Some swear that she built the whole house alone. "In four months at that!" Mias, her brother who completed his schooling in 1927 and then left, said that the house was completed when their father died in 1926. Some last touches had to be done to the gables. This, Lenie managed. And following Kloof custom, everyone lent a hand when someone was building. A cement *bankie* (bench) like a wide step is built onto a side wall. Mischievous

Kloovers say Lenie built it "specially for Willem to sit on while lazing the days away". In midsummer heat it was custom to sit outside and move a chair around following the shade. She attached Willem's bankie to the wall "so that he could at least lift his backside when the sun scorched him".

Dr Bart du Toit who wrote a thesis about the Kloovers describes Lenie as a specialist in her own right. Apart from her medical knowledge she was very sociable compared with her quiet and modest husband. Where Lenie helped out in many ways up and down the Valley, Willem spent most of his time in and around the house.

Lenie was a much-talked about person in her lifetime. Legendary after her death.

A forester, Herholdt, met her on the road one day, sickle in hand, knapsack on her back and the sweat pouring down her face!

"Aunt Lenie where're you going? And in this stifling midday heat?" he asked.

"My boy! Your uncle Willem has such *sawwerige handjies* (softish hands) and *eelterige boude* (callousy buttocks) that I went to work in the vineyards myself. Believe me! Today my own two buttocks are freckled."

In the 1960s Lenie went to Dr Ben Swart in Oudtshoorn to have a hysterectomy.

She was admitted, operated on and Ben kept her in hospital for 12 days to recuperate taking her restlessness into account.

It was arranged beforehand that Willem would fetch her on a specific date, day and hour.

One day in the Kloof, however, is much like the next with seasons more important than dates.

No-one arrived.

She took her suitcase and walked from Oudtshoorn hospital to the market where the dilapidated, rickety Prince Albert bus always waited.The bus took to the road in rainy weather. Up Swartberg Pass to Gamkaskloof turn-off where it stopped. She got off and walked the remaining 57 km home. The mountain streams were swollen and she often had to wade through water up to her armpits.

"Doctor, you won't believe me," she told Ben later, "sometimes I was so tired that I keeled over. Then I regained consciousness and carried on."

She left hospital early morning. She arrived home in the dark that night.

"And the Kloovers end the story: 'She outlived Willem.'"

In retrospect, the stories treat Willem too niggardly. Arguably it was his "misfortune" to have married a live-wire woman. Lenie was a mercurial personality and Willem's tranquil nature contrasted strongly. People who knew them well say he was a dependable, stable and non-excitable personality. Lenie was a complete extrovert. Where she went there was fun and laughter. "She could create a story out of a mundane incident and give it a delightful twist."

The fact is, Lenie was versatile — sick comforter, teacher for a term once when there was no-one else, florist, baker, dressmaker and tailor of stylish suits for men.

Cutting up meat was another specialty, be it sheep, porker, goat or buck. She made *boerseep* (soap) which she cut up into bricks. And whoever tasted *moskonfyt* (grape syrup) made by Lenie knew that no other could compare with hers.

When the Kloof started emptying in the 1980s, Lenie moved to Prince Albert. The change was not easy. For Lenie the townfolk "simply didn't get up in the mornings." The only one who fitted her definition of "morning" was the Dutch baker who started working at four a.m.

One morning when he arrived, Lenie was already waiting for him, *opgedollie* (dolled up) and ready for the day. The baker asked: "*Tant* Lenie, you worked so hard all your life, why don't you rest now?"

Lenie's answer is now classic Kloof: "Look here, young fellow! I told my daughter that when I die they must bury me quickly because I want to start spooking immediately!"

Another unforgettable Kloof personality was Johann Kellerman.

He was an *inkommer* after the road when everyone had transportation. Bakkies and cars which traversed the formidable Kloof route had many more problems than Martiens Snyman's little Morris which was always diagnosed with "coil trouble".

A mechanic was sorely needed.

Someone remembered about Johann Kellerman. He married a Mostert girl from the Kloof and also had a thorough knowledge of cars and their engines. Johann agreed to leave the garage in Worcester where he worked. He kept Kloof cars on the road and never charged a cent for his work. When anyone asked: "How much do I owe you, Johann?" he would say: "*Ag wat*! Leave me a few potatoes."

The "few potatoes" came in the form of meat, vegetables, fruit or lucerne for his animals.

"You see," Kloovers explain "he was a cripple and couldn't farm much. His young brother-in-law moved in with them to help with the tiny farm. Anyway, he was far too busy with motor cars to do much else."

It is not only Kloovers who have vivid memories of the past but *inkommers* as well. Like Margaret Stoddard.

In the late 1950s Margaret's photographic studio in Oudtshoorn "was commissioned by the authorities to go and snap the Kloovers for their Identity Documents," she starts the tale.

"The new wide road to The Hell was only a thought and we had to take the narrow route."

In the dark of morning Margaret, her four children, Jan du Toit a professional photographer, and a few friends negotiated Die Leer. "Inch by inch on that terrible route, for one misstep, and you would fall into forever! Just like that with your eyes open you crash into Hell!"

Their housemaid Sielie knew stories from her *voormense* about The Hell. "*As djille oppie pad Hel toe Die Oog sien, gat vriestalike dinge met djille gabeer.*" (Literally: If you, on the road to Hell, see The Eye, terrible things will happen to you.)

When they looked up in the dark of early morning they saw the eye which shone down brightly on them. Just like Sielie said: '*n Groot en hiller oog wat ytie hiemel afkyk na mense wat Hel toe gaat. Djille sal wiet dissie Oog want hy's groterder en annerster as anner sterre.*" (Literally: A big and bright eye which looks down from heaven on people going to Hell. You'll know its The Eye because it's bigger than and different from other stars.)

Even after their precarious climb, Margaret thought The Hell was heaven on earth. "Simply beautiful! A wonderful place!" she said.

"The air was clean and fresh. Plenty of trees. Babbling brooks and streams, and hundreds upon hundreds of birds flying or singing. Peaceful! Heavenly quiet!"

Their long walk started. To Middelplaas School. Over Kleinberg. The first house.

Margaret continues: "Near the house is a man. He stands motionless on the roadside. He wears an *ouma brilletjie* (granny glasses). His gaze penetrates. I'm terrified but I scold myself: 'Sielie, be damned! Margaret, stop this nonsense!'"

Hazel, Margaret's eldest child says: "Ma, it's a ghost! Sielie said terrible things would happen to us!" Thereafter everyone was nervous. Margaret tried to save the situation.

"There are no such things as ghosts! *A nee a!* Enough is enough." She admits: "I had quite a battle trying to get the fear out of myself. It stayed!"

Then they encountered "huge, terrible-looking red locusts and every time one flew up in front of us we had the fright of our lives."

"We walked and we walked. The day was getting hot. Another house.

"I'm also incredibly inquisitive," she admits. "I walk to the house and peep in through the window. In the middle of the floor there's a brand-new yellowwood coffin. A coldness takes hold of me. I trot away whistling so that you can hear me way over there! Like the old folks did when they passed a graveyard. But I tell you! The devil could not have frightened me more than the silence in The Hell." Everything seemed suffocatingly quiet. As if something ominous was stalking me.

"Then he appeared the second time. That staring man. Dressed like the first ghost, long pants, khaki shirt, suspenders, hat on his head and *ouma brilletjie*. He leaned on a long *kierie* (walking-stick) and stared quietly at us. His eyes seemed to burn into my soul.

"Let's cut a long story short," says Margaret. "We saw that ghost five times on the way to Middelplaas. By the fifth time I was at ease. I even wanted to greet him with a hankey wrapped round my hand so as not to get ghost burn, and say, 'Good day, old chap! Why don't you rest?' But I decided not to be disrespectful to the late Mr So and So."

"So I walked on."

Eventually, they arrived at the school, took the photographs and in the afternoon started their 15 kilometre hike back to the Cordiers at Kleinberg who had not been "snapped" yet.

Then nightfall overtook them.

"Never in my life," says Margaret, "have I prayed harder that a photo taken in lantern light should come out. Otherwise we would have had to come back.

"In the dark we started our return journey up Die Leer. The Cordiers lit our way with two lanterns as best they could.

"I had blisters on my feet, I was dogtired and was hit by the full meaning of the word *despondency*. The children were missing! Everyone but I was certain they were already waiting on top. I shouted for them, my voice echoing over the Kloof. Close to tears I said: Be damned everything! If I fall to my death, leave me in Hell! I'll be in the right place!"

But all's well that ends well. The trip was a success, the "lantern photo's" came out well.

And the ghosts? They were Kloof men. One of the buyers apparently went shopping for everyone for the photo session and they stood waiting for the photographers to pass before following them.

Chapter eleven
Koos Uil/Kleinkoos/Rooi Koos/
Koos Road-builder

The Koos Owl/Small Koos/Red Koos/Koos Road-builder mentioned above is one and the same person and has the distinction that a monument was erected in honour of him because he made The Hell accessible. He had made a road straight to Hell!

Koos van Zyl is the man who had the courage to make what might be the most dangerous road in South Africa; the winding road to Gamkaskloof and the nerve-racking downroad into the Kloof.

"Many a time he almost *donnered, stootskraper en al, gat oor kop, Die Hel in.*" (Literally: Tumbled bulldozer and all backside over head into The Hell.)

Koos is not only a road-maker who made history with his Allis Chalmers bulldozer, he recorded the daily happening in pencil on paper in his home-made caravan by candle and lamplight. He obviously has a sense of history. And he's a poet to boot!

He started his tale in the third person.

"The honest, hard-working farmers of Gamkaskloof had no road to take out their products. The only route was by donkey via Bo- or Onderpoort to Prince Albert or Calitzdorp.

"After persistent representations to Dr Otto du Plessis, the Administrator of the Cape, he arrived on horseback one day, through Bopoort where Gamka Dam is today, and 18 farmers met him. He made a speech and promised that a road would be built. Then followed a feast like only the Kloovers can offer with a *vleisbraai* (barbeque) and a dance.

"In November 1959, the Divisional Council of Prince Albert received permission from the Administrator to start with the road. It would be 90 per cent bulldozing and 10 per cent blasting." Divisional Councils were responsible for roads in the Cape Province at the time.

Koos van Zyl was a young bachelor and worked for the Divisional Council. At that stage he did not dream of fame as a road-builder to The Hell.

Titch Reilly was the engineer in charge of roads. He realised that no more than a negotiable road was needed, not a highway with gradients and so forth.

Klein Koos Uil had all the qualifications, the grit and he could maintain discipline. Titch asked him to take up the challenge.

"In November 1959 my Allis and I took the road up Swartberg Pass. That formidable pass! The bulldozer could not be transported and I drove up. I towed my caravan. The bends are short and the pass much too steep for a large vehicle to piggy-back the Allis.

"This was a small foretaste of things to come."

Titch had instructed him "to take the shortest route. When you come to a *koppie* (hillock) go round, left or right whichever is the shorter."

Thereafter Titch, by his own testimony, visited the site once a month and left the rest in Koos's hands.

Just before the summit of the Swartberg Pass there was a turn-off to a forestry station called Kliphuisvlei. That's where Koos wished to commence the road. But on his way he met a very suspicious forester. "He stopped me," says Koos, "and asked if he could inspect my machine! And the caravan.

"'Of course,' said I.

"He looked and he poked, even went right into my little caravan," Koos continued.

158

"'Do you have any "defence"?' he asked euphemistically.

"'If you mean a gun, yes, I have one,' I replied.

"'You know you're not to use guns on state property,' he admonished."

Koos realised that this man thought he was "a common poacher".

He explained that he was there to make a road to The Hell. "I've a team of workmen following. There are *tiers* in these mountains and I have to protect them!"

The forester was not convinced.

"I got mad as hell," admits Koos, "and I said I would go back where I came from and he could explain to the authorities. And to hell with the road!"

The forester changed his tune but warned: "You know we count all the buck once a month and heaven help you if there's one missing!"

"Well," laughs Koos, "I do not remember how many buck we shot for the pot but I do know that their counting leaves much to be desired!"

Koos started the road at Kliphuisvlei and recorded: "Easy terrain. Not dangerous at all. I could comfortably complete a mile a month. One of my stations was called Kiewedoor-se-Werf (Kievedoor's yard). There we were plagued by a loner baboon.

"He would wait until we left and then visit our camp. He would take a handful of sugar from one, potatoes from another and so on. Once he put his head into a flour bag and came up with a snow-white face.

"We decided to surprise him. One morning we left as usual but once out of sight, we surrounded the site. Before he realised it, he was in trouble. The labourers were first-rate stone throwers and they pelted him mercilessly. He climbed into a tree where he was an easier target. When it became too much

159

even for a tough baboon to bear, he let go, landed on all fours and confronted them with threateningly barks: 'HUW! HUW!'

"You should have seen those brave warriors! They scattered in all directions, fell over one another, got up and ran for cover shouting: 'Help! Help!'"

That was the end of baboon visits.

The team moved camp as the work demanded. They moved to Van Zyl's Drif. It was named after Koos but it's an "honour" he would rather forget. They moved in the late afternoon. It was almost dark.

The labourers decided it was too late to erect their huts. They put the corrugated iron sheets against a rock which formed a lean-to cover for the night.

Koos joined them with his *potjiekos* to be cooked on their fire.

"We sat chatting round the fire. On small veld stools. Everyone was a good talker."

Koos carries on with the story: "In mid-sentence one stopped. Then everyone kept quiet. We listened. We heard someone approaching. Closer and closer. We heard his footsteps and his clothes brushing against the branches.

"Stoffel Botes said: 'Who can this be?'

"I said: 'I don't know. Maybe a Kloover wanting to know how the road is coming on.'

"We waited. The visitor had to come into the circle of the firelight. Nothing happened. Only the eerie, tense and ominous silence.

"The labourers, their nerves in tatters, jumped up and disappeared under their lean-to.

"I sat for a few moments longer, then I too turned tail and sprinted to my caravan. I slammed the door shut behind me.

"Ashamed of my fear, I bravely shouted: 'If you want to frighten me come forward. Otherwise I'll shoot!'

"Silence! To this day no-one can explain what happened."

(Koos obviously did not know about the Dutchman who follows hikers. Or maybe he does not believe in this ghost.)

"We moved to Kareekloof; a lovely valley with an abundance of water flowing in rivulets down the mountain slopes.

"One morning a scared labourer woke me around four o'clock wanting to know what kind of animal was in the camp. They could not see him. Only hear him.

"The next moment I heard the GE-ARG! GE-ARG! sound of a leopard. Not wanting to alarm my colleagues, I said it sounded like a porcupine.

"He looked at me in disbelief. 'It sounds like a *tier!*'

"'Then why ask me?' I replied.

"The following day I had to cross a river on a late afternoon quest for meat for our supper. And there, on the dry stones in the river-bed were the clear, wet footprints of a huge leopard. I ran! And needless to say that night we had a meatless supper.

"Once four workers wanted to borrow my axe. There are beautiful *olien* (wild olive) trees suitable for *kieries* in the nearby kloof.

"I felt up to mischief. So I followed them quietly.

"They chattered like birds, carefree and happy.

"Then I grunted: 'GE-ARG! GE-ARG!' And growled from my nearby hiding place.

"They stopped and listened. Heard nothing more and chopped again.

"Then I let go!

"They flung the axe down and took to their heels, shouting: *'Tier! Tier!'*

"Later at the camp I reminded them that they had borrowed my axe and I needed it.

"Shamefacedly they admitted how they had been

terrified by a very threatening *tier* and had run for their lives.

"'Go and fetch it immediately! I need it! Now!' I demanded with a straight face.

"They pleaded. They begged. They explained, until I showed them the axe which I had picked up and brought back and we all had a good laugh."

From Kareekloof onwards the going was tougher. The mountainside was steep and sloped down. The ground was much harder.

"We passed Doringkloof and tackled the last mountain before coming to Gamkaskloof when we saw a beehive. One of the workers decided he wanted honey, but the bees tackled him. I had to dig into my emergency medicine chest to ease his suffering.

"Also in Kareekloof I noticed that a leopard spoor invariably follows the donkey filly, never the adult. I've often wondered how they know the difference.

"From Doringkloof on to Perdekraal also known as Langnek.

"A friend came to visit me on site. I realised I was building a road to a place I had never seen. So we decided to walk to Gamkaskloof. We entered from Seweweekspoort down Die Leer. Neither one of us was used to this type of hiking and climbing, and my feet were covered in blisters.

"We stopped at the first house. It belonged to Johannes Mostert who shared it with his beautiful daughter Marie. Then and there I decided this was the girl I wanted to marry. Instantly, I concluded that my feet were much too sore to carry on and asked if we could stay over with them.

"They were most interested in the road-building and we had a happy weekend. And many more after that. Until Marie and I were eventually married.

"From Perdekraal the route was rapidly downhill to Elandspad. The slopes were very steep and the mountainside rockhard. We had to use explosives.

"One Monday morning — we were fetched on Fridays and brought back on Mondays — the lorry had just dropped us off and had returned to Prince Albert when my roadworks machine broke down. I would have to wait until Friday before anyone could remedy the matter.

"That was quite unacceptable.

"I asked Piet, one of the workers, to accompany me to the nearest farmhouse in Gamkaskloof where I could telephone for help.

"Tuesday morning we had a good, solid breakfast. I put on a new overall and my strong leather lumber jacket. And we set off. We had to find our own route.

"The area was densely covered in shrub like the thorny wild asparagus called *katdoring* and the *haak-en-steek* (Acasia heteracantha) umbrella-thorn tree.

"We just could not get through.

"We decided to try crossing the mountain, but came to a place where we could go no further.

"Back to the thorny scrub.

"Piet kept complaining that the branches pushed his hat over his eyes.

"'Man, be thankful! Now you can't see the horrors we're negotiating!' was all the sympathy he got.

"'*Ja*! And if a *tier* stands in front of me? Then I can't even see him.'

"'Look, man! If this happens, look him in the eye then quickly pull your hat down again and you won't see him anymore!' I advised.

"We came to a waterfall, four feet high. A wooden pole — obviously useless — was the means by which earlier travellers had slid down.

"I jumped down.

"Piet balked! 'I can't swim!'

"'Damn it, man! I'll catch you. You won't have to swim.'

"'No!' said Piet stubbornly and stood where he stood.

"I begged! I pleaded! Then I lost my temper!

"'Well you can damn well stay up there and *vrek*!" (Crudity for die.)

"Piet jumped and I got him out safely.

"Eventually, we came to an orchard full of ripe *naartjies* and oranges. We were ravenous. We had had nothing to eat after breakfast. Then we saw the man with the gun pointed at us.

"I explained! He offered assistance and we went with him.

"Then I looked at my clothes. My brand-new overall and treasured leather jacket were in tatters. I had to use the remnants of the jacket as pants to make myself look presentable.

"I phoned the Divisional Council and we went back.

"Once at Elandspad one of the labourers fell down a krantz of about 30 m. He was taken to hospital where he was X-rayed but, fortunately, not seriously injured.

"Koos wrote a poem about this incident starting:
"Die volkies dink mos hulle is tuff
en duik sommer van die kranse af!"
(The people think they are very tough
And dive from the krantzes.)"

Koos relates this and many other incidents in verse in which he tells how he was forced to consider another route "unless they wish to bring a corpse from below."

"So if the council wants to be wise
they will listen to good advice
and build the road the other *kant* (side)
Even on the footpath *rant* (edge)."

Despite his poetry, his thoughts and "advice", Koot continued bulldozing this downhill stretch from Elandspad into The Hell where he nearly lost his own life on at least two occasions.

About 4,8 km remained to be bulldozed.

Koos says: "A giant rock hung in our way and refused to budge. I put the blade under the rock to pry it loose. No result. I pushed! I bumped! No result. I put the machine in reverse to attempt another push when that rock fell.

"Now you must appreciate the fact that my Allis weighs 14 tons. The rock landed on the forepart and lifted the back sky-high.

"I sat helpless in midair.

"What to do? The machine was in reverse gear and it vibrated furiously. Eventually this saved me. The momentum caused the rock to move gradually until it tilted towards the precipice. When it finally fell, the machine almost followed.

"That was a close shave.

"The second time a rock dislodged right above me. I saw it and in a flash changed to reverse gear. The rock came thundering down and just, just missed falling onto the cabin where I sat.

"That was when I realised I was also gambling with my own life. 'This is life-threatening work!' I said to myself."

Theo Olwage was teaching in The Hell at the time Koos was working on this part of the road. He recalls how terrifying and awe-inspiring it was. "Even to stand and watch him was nerve-fraying," said Theo.

"Many a time the only way he could brake this massive machine and stop it from falling *gat-oor-kop* (head over hells) was to dig the blade in.

"One day the route was so steep he weighed the back of the bulldozer down with rocks so that the

165

chains could get a grip on the surface. Even then he needed the blade as an additional brake."

At this stage Koos realised that not only was he risking his machine and his own life, but the lives of his working companions.

He recorded what followed in verse which he called "Die Padmaker se Lied" (Song of the Road-Builder).

It relates how the Council promised, but never delivered, until the day Koos lost his temper, jumped into his car and when he walked into the offices when he should have been working no-one could understand why he was there. He said they paid too little.

"*Ek waag my lewe daar vir noual meer dan 'n jaar.*" (I have risked my life for a year and more.)

He would complete the road for R550. He would not argue if they wished to replace him with a better operator. "If he has a wish to break his neck!"

Koos's equipment for the pioneering task was very poor indeed.

No gravy train treatment. Ordinary pay.

He even had to supply his own caravan. He described it as "a home made of hardboard. It was mounted on a two-wheel Hobard welding machine under-carriage. There was no nose-wheel. "I replaced this with a 200 litre oil drum.

"Inside it was so cramped that a bed just fitted in on the 'wide' side."

High up on the Swartberg Mountain the southerly winds can blow fiercely.

One night Koos was sound asleep after another hard day's work, totally oblivious of the elements.

"The next morning he wanted to fill his coffee kettle outside at the stream when he nearly stepped out into eternity.

"During the night the wind must have moved the

'nose wheel' drum and the caravan to the edge of the precipice."

Koos says: "The District Council could not hear what I thought about my working conditions. Only the veld and the sky bore me witness."

The stretch of the road which falls a thousand metres in a few kilometres, was completed in 1962 by Koos and eight labourers. Looking at it from Elandspas it seems impossible that this fearsome, zig-zagging dirt road could be negotiated by any vehicle, let alone a bulldozer.

Many a meek driver had a temporary nervous breakdown on entering by car and Kloovers had to drive the distressed motorists out when their courage totally collapsed.

Koos is also a philosopher. He penned the phrase: "This road to Hell was made with good intentions."

All that remained was the upgrading and widening of the road through Gamkaskloof. Even this was eventful.

At Kaffirskloof Koos had a memorable visit.

The Marais family brought an old man, Broekman Botes, to see the bulldozer. They had told him of the size and immense power of the machine.

He wanted to see for himself if this was possible.

"*Oom* Broekman got off the donkey cart and cautiously approached 'the evil thing' with its 'evil power'.

"I switched the machine off," recorded Koos, "and stepped down. We shook hands. He asked if this monster could truly uproot three or four huge thorn trees. I promised I would show him.

"Then he walked round the machine, still very suspicious. He looked at the chain grips and said: 'Heavens! There is even room for people to sit here.'

"I explained that those were 'wheels'. That he refused to believe.

"'Wheels are round! And that's that!'

"He moved to the back where the ripper was. I explained that it worked like a plough.

"This angered him. 'Do you take me for a child? That thing is two feet above the ground. It cannot bend!'

"I tried to explain the action but *oom* Broekman shook his head.

"He left in complete disbelief saying: 'This is a thing of the devil that you have brought into Gamkaskloof.'

"And he left mumbling that if his poor dead father and poor dead mother had to see what that evil devil was up to in the Kloof, they would turn in their graves."

When Koos tackled the inside road, he courted Marie Mostert seriously. Most of his weekends were spent at her home.

Marie, and her father — her mother had died — lived in the old *opstal* (farmhouse), and her brother Willem and his family lived in the school at Boplaas which they had adapted to their needs.

Between Gamka River and Boplaas there's a farm called Midland.

The woman who used to live there had died and it is said she had had "a vile temper and tongue, and used to scream and shout at the poor children at the drop of a hat."

Willem Mostert told Koos that Midland was haunted. The old woman's ghost could often be heard at midnight, screaming, shouting and swearing. He warned Koos to stop working past the midnight hour.

"I had to pass this place on my way home," says Koos. "Willem repeatedly warned me that it was very risky.

"This did not worry me at all. I kept working until late into the dark hours and never gave the ghost another thought.

168

"Until one night!

"I worked until well near midnight. I walked home past Midland. Dog-tired and craving a smoke, I drew a match to light my pipe. The trees on either side of the road form a tunnel. Dense thorn trees.

"My watch beeped the midnight hour. I struck a match and then that ghost started screaming! It penetrated through bone and marrow!

"I ran! Brother! I ran until my lungs burnt.

"'Hell, man! You can't be so scared' I tried to calm myself. I stopped! Took out my pipe in another attempt to light it. At the second draw that woman let go more furiously than before.

"That's when nothing, absolutely nothing could stop me. I bolted like a bat out of hell and did not stop until I was indoors, safe and sound.

"That weekend at Marie's I was quiet and subdued. I wasn't going to admit to a soul that I was terrified of their ghost. Willem least of all.

"Sunday afternoon Marie and I went for a long walk and in a moment of weakness I told her about my experience. But I asked her not to tell her brother.

"The next weekend I arrived as usual and Willem was there greeting me with a disgraceful obscenity. 'Why the hell didn't you tell me about the ghost? It wasn't a *verdomde* (damned) ghost it was one of my best *bokkapaters* (goats) which hung himself in one of the thorn trees. I might have saved him if you'd opened your mouth!'

"Fat lot I cared about his damn goat." Koos ended this tale. "It will teach him to frighten his future brother-in-law with stories of haunted houses and ghosts!"

It transpired that the goat had been standing up against the thorn tree stretching higher and higher to get to the topmost juicy leaves when his front paws must have slipped and lodged in the fork of the tree.

What Koos had to endure for his people — after he had married Marie, he became a Kloover for a while — he felt he had done a very necessary job. He succeeded in easing their lives and enabled them to improve their economy.

Koos ended his tale honestly and very simply: "There is no valley more beautiful than Gamkaskloof!"

Koos van Zyl and his wife Marie, née Mostert,
and their first-born, Marianne.
(Photograph: Marie Lilienfeld)

Chapter twelve
After the road

"Next time I will stop my car in front of the school!" This was the promise made by Dr Otto du Plessis in 1959 when he announced that a road would be built to Gamkaskloof.

When he said this, he was sitting on a snow-white horse named Venus and was being honoured with a 21-gun salute. The road was named after him.

The day of the opening was only the second time in the history of the Kloof that a VIP had visited there. There were also some one hundred residents and the Kloovers gave themselves a two-day public holiday.

Dr du Plessis died just before the ceremony and his successor, Dr Nico Malan, did the honours with Mrs Beatrice du Plessis attending.

The weather did not play along and it poured with rain.

Piet Botha, a Divisional Councillor, started the proceedings saying: "As a well-established SAP (South African Party member) it is my privilege to lead all you Nats (Nationalist Party members) into Hell."

When the laughter subsided, one of the Kloover's drily remarked: "And even all the Sappe are *nat* (wet) today.

Piet explained how the road cost only £5 000 and how the "inside road" had been shortened to 15 miles from Elandspas to Die Leer. Little did the beneficiaries foresee that this road, which was built with

171

such good intentions, would cause the valley to bleed to death within three decades. Or did they?

Dr Malan warned that a road "was wonderful but it could empty a farm or even a small town."

Most of the Kloovers resented these words believing it would never happen to them.

That evening there was merry-making as only Kloovers could do it. The school at Middelplaas, where Marina Ehlers still taught one girl and two boys, was festively decorated and was the centre of the fun.

Sixteen guests from outside the Kloof (quite a few were journalists) attended the party. It was still pouring but the small candles in small glasses on the school desks and the general atmosphere of the room gave it warmth and put life and camaraderie into the fun.

Two sheep and three goats were prepared for the braai.

Lenie Marais supplied 15 sweet yeast loaves of bread.

Willem Joubert with his concertina and Piet Mostert on guitar made music.

Everything was so much fun that Koot Cordier braved the duck weather and went on horseback — seven miles there and seven miles back — to bring his concertina.

Marina Ehlers and Piet Joubert were the *voordansers* (lead dancers) and *die stof het gestaan* (dust was kicked up).

It was *deurdruk dagbreek toe* (press on till dawn). The joy was immeasurable. Gone were the days of solitude and isolation when the outside world did not concern the Kloovers.

Kloovers thought they would continue living in their own private kingdom, no matter that they trailed behind the development of the outside world. They would be able to go out when they pleased and

172

"even the ambulance could now get in." Furthermore, their children in surrounding schools could spend weekends at home.

Not a soul thought that they would turn their backs on a unique era in their lives. Or that a brand-new historical phase had started which would introduce before and after-the-road eras.

But most importantly, no-one foresaw the influx of *inkommers* who would descend on them. Tourism and tourists were foreign words and perceptions. If the Kloovers had any idea of the politicizing which had preceded the road, they did not avoid it. They were "entitled to better communication with outside areas" was their logical conclusion. After all, they paid taxes like everyone else.

If they thought or knew that the Calitzdorpers had lobbied for the road for personal or selfish reasons, it did not weigh heavily.

It is undeniable that the well-to-do and influential farmers would benefit tremendously by a dam in Gamka River. The fact is, the dam cut off the best route for many Kloovers.

The cost of the road and a causeway of £8 000 across Gamka to connect Bo and Onderplaas was small change compared with the benefits of the dam water used for irrigation farming.

The only transport which came into the Kloof in earlier times was the Morris and a *bokwa* (buck-wagon). The *bokwa* can still be seen under a tree near Hannes Mostert's home.

Hannes pioneered transport after the road.

Earlier, when there were still donkey trains, he met farmers at the top of Die Leer and conveyed their products to the station. Although his Diamond T-lorry was parked in "the tin house", Hannes could, in future, stop outside the farmer's house and transport the whole family to their destinations and back.

Although Kloovers paid for this, it was not at all to their liking. Many decided it was too expensive to pay for transportation. They were a proud and self-reliant people who did not like to ask someone else to do their jobs for them. Henk Mostert openly said he disliked asking people to bring his children home from school and take them back again. Even if he paid for their service.

Koot Cordier was equally stiff-necked and independent. He never drove his own bakkie. Would not or could not? But a bakkie he bought and someone drove it.

For him "it was different from getting into someone else's car." In his vehicle he was the boss.

Hannes Nefdt was the first to bring in a tractor. It stood under the thorn trees and "quite soon the tyres were tattered and torn."

Money was no problem. Kloovers simply pulled out the *trommels* (trunks) and counted out "the change" they always put there after transactions with the shopkeepers or vendors.

"The Kloover's had money," says Zannie van der Walt, "not necessarily because they saved, but because they never spent it."

"Those people had no idea how much money was put in the *trommels* through the years."

It is said that Piet Mostert worried about his "loose money" after the road. When he decided to move to "town", he asked his daughter who worked at a bank to "count and deposit it". By then the country had switched to "the rand and cent system" and the old blue and red notes amounted to £50 000.

Children realised their parents were not poor. They had suffered poverty through the years and got by with bare necessities. They were raised with the idea that money was something to be put in a *trommel*. It had very little place in their lives.

After the road, they realised that money had value. Vehicles cost money, petrol cost money and cost-of-living became a factor. Bartering was out, "money-in-the-hand-commerce" was in.

Children no longer walked to and from school. They were fetched and taken.

Kloovers realised their farms were actually "rather small". To afford their new lifestyle they needed more land and they started buying out departing neighbour's farms.

One of the biggest land transactions took place in the 1980s when "The Doctors" bought farms.

Drs T Allwright, F Henk Badenhorst, André de V Louw and H Roelof van Huyssteen bought Kleinberg.

The depopulation of the Kloof worried them and they wished to restore and conserve this unique place for future generations.

Kleinberg mountain forms the western boundary of Gamkaskloof. To the west is the farm Kleinberg with a small but fertile valley of about 2 km. There are caves alongside the perennial river where Bushmen paintings and figure printing can be seen.

This section of Gamkaskloof probably has the most breathtakingly beautiful and picturesque mountain scenery.

From the floor of the valley named Leeukloof one looks up at massive mountain peaks, the highest being Blouberg (1 880 m) which is criss-crossed by deep ravines and sculptured krantz formations.

In winter months the *Aloe ferox* is spectacular with its flaming flowers covering the mountainsides.

On the northern side there is a steep krantz. Oshoek River flows perenially and gives life to the otherwise arid Karoo soil. The peak is called Prammetjie (vulgarism for breast). Below is a dilapidated barn which points to the top of the 900 m-long Die Leer. There an old barn was formerly used to store dried fruit and other products.

From there the mountain road turns west across a plateaux. After about 12 km it joins the Bosluis-kloof road.

Some folks believe Kleinberg was the original farm in Gamkaskloof. Others maintain Baviaans-kloof alongside the Gamka River was the first. Many know "for a fact that the Cordiers lived on Kleinberg long before Petrus David Swanepoel applied for ownership in 1883."

It was in this area that Deneys Reitz was hosted.

When the doctors bought the farm there were two ramshackle houses. The first built by the original Cordier and the other by his son. There is a stone ruin which might have been an old *bokkraal* (goat enclosure) and a threshing floor with a five metre diameter. Below Piet Mostert's house there is a tussock of Agave shrub on the grave of *tant* Lientjie Cordier.

The river supplies domestic water and water for a small mill. The original house at Kleinberg had five small rooms. The kitchen was not connected to the *voorhuis*. About 800 m upstream someone had built a cement and soil irrigation furrow.

For 20 years no-one farmed at Kleinberg.

The style of the house is similar to the rest in the valley. The construction is basically stone mixed with "grass". The walls were "plastered" with clay or mud. In some cases frames in a different shade of clay were added.

The foundations are made of clay. The walls are 30 to 40 cm thick and the glassless windows are covered by wooden shutters. Stable doors were made of roughly finished wood and seldom fitted properly. At Kleinberg stones which are plentiful, were used for walls. The walls are about 2 m high and the ceilings and roofs the same as in other Kloof homes.

The *voorkamer* (3 x 4 m) is connected to the main bedroom by a door. An inside window opening connects this to the second bedroom which has an outside door. The kitchen was separate.

Next to the kitchen is a small pantry where an inside door leads to a third bedroom.

There seems to have been no stove only a *vuurherd* (open fireplace) 2 m long. There was no bathroom.

Dr P C Luttig (he later turned blind), a general practitioner at Prince Albert between 1901 and 1932, dictated an experience of a trip to Kleinberg to his wife.

"The going is very rough, big loose stones, rough gravel, coarse sand, long stretches of water and rock to climb over. At times one has to go along the steep, awkward mountain path to avoid cliffs or deep pools of water.

"It is impossible to go in by any other means, except footslogging or on horseback. Our direction is due south for about two miles when the course of the river turns north-west for about half a mile, then south again.

"At this point we are struck by the awesome sight of the tremendous rocks of quartzite piled up to heights of thousands of feet in massive formation. At this point the river turns for the second time, the amount of rocks is most impressive and fills one with awe. Here the mountain seems sliced off like a piece of bread showing a surface certainly half a mile long and a thousand feet high."

He gives his own version of the "explosions" at Skietkrans.

"When the wind blows from a certain direction, this cliff gives a peculiar echo very much like a series of explosions of dynamite or canon roar. Hence it is called Skietkrans.

"To the observant eye two large black eagles will usually be seen floating in the blue sky above this cliff, apparently watchful of the happenings below.

"Their nest will probably be found in one of the crevices in the face of the cliffs. One wonders what prey they have carried up to their mysterious home. Even a human baby could not be rescued from this perilous situation, should it become a victim.

"As we proceed further down the river bed, we came to a place where the whole surface is strewn with huge boulders from one side to the other. With great difficulty one finds a place where a pedestrian or a horse can get through to the opposite side.

"Another dangerous factor on this journey is quicksand. Once after visiting a patient there, I had the nasty experience of feeling my horse disappear under me up to his neck in a pool of quicksand.

"I went sprawling over his head, fortunately with no serious result. The poor dumb, shivering animal, well accustomed to these episodes, managed to struggle out and we were able to continue our eventful journey."

Before the last Kloovers left the valley, the doctors had already restored two houses. They and their guests frequently visit Kleinberg. The doctors wanted to buy the rest of Gamkaskloof but it was zoned as agricultural land and legalities were complex and almost prohibitive.

The doctors compromised and the Department of Nature Conservation took over most of the forestry land.

At the time, Kobus du Plessis, head of Nature Conservation, anticipated hiking trails to all parts of The Hell which was to become a living museum with orchards, vineyards, *karrie* to be brewed and the home industries of years gone by "resurrected".

"We want the Kloof to be alive! Living!" he said when the transaction was completed.

Together with the doctors, it is run as a nature reserve and forms part of the greater Zwartberg Nature Reserve with headquarters at Oudtshoorn.

Zannie van der Walt was appointed resident Conservation Officer assisted by his wife Anita. Shortly after their appointment, a camping site was erected on the site of Lewies (Soothsayer) Nel's house. Lenie Marais's cottage was restored as a guest house, and Zannie and Anita work and live in the Swanepoel house.

It was decided to restore a further three houses as overnight facilities for *voetslaners* (hikers).

At the start of the millennium, if and when money is available, facilities for a 6 km route with interpretation points will be established.

Anglers are not forgotten with planned facilities along the Gamka River which will have to be cleared of reeds.

The two school buildings are destined to become cultural historical points grandly referred to as 'Interpretation Centres'. This is where schoolchildren and students will be able to learn about the flora and fauna typical of Gamkaskloof; and much more. The enormous variety of natural flora is not always noticed by the uniniated eye. It has to be pointed out. The *spekboom* for instance is said to be unique to the area.

There is almost a "crowded" presence of fauna resulting in over-grazing on the northern slopes. The grey *reebok* and *klipspringers* particularly abound.

Because of the abundant water, facilities for swimming will be investigated.

Gamka River is the breeding place for eagles and other krantz-nesting birds. Also on the list of future projects is a route by donkey or donkey cart and a "small bus" for disabled visitors in order to control traffic.

The third, albeit small property compared with the total Kloof area, is that of Annetjie and Bennie Joubert. They have restored four family homes including those of Annetjie's grandfather *oupa* Henk Mostert and her father Piet Mostert.

These delightful cottages are used as guest houses.

Annetjie was the prime propagator of The Hell as tourist attraction. In the 1960s, soon after the road had been opened, she saw what was happening and realised that the Kloof could be kept "alive" by Inkommers.

As a Mostert and a Cordier descendant, with all the family stories well remembered and nurtured, she cannot be more indigenous.

Their farms are shaded by a variety of trees; a hefty stone's throw from the Gamka River.

This section is a paradise for nature lovers, particularly the caves and Bushman paintings and reasonably easy hiking routes.

Annetjie visualises a holistic approach to a holiday in The Hell, starting long before entering the Kloof itself.

"Start your visit when going up the Swartberg mountain," she advises. "It's part of the total experience and the complete route is part of the beauty of a visit to The Hell.

Annetjie's progressive dreaming started shortly after the road had been inaugurated and up to 50 cars visited the Kloof per weekend.

However, her insights were not shared by the rest of the Kloovers. They experienced the road as a necessary evil. Their privacy was shattered.

Nosy Parkers arrived at front and back doors often at impossible times "to see for ourselves how you people live!"

A typical example after the umpteenth such incident was a visit to the house of Andreas and Sankie Marais. Their house was an easy target; clearly visible from the road.

An unnamed journalist describes the incident which took place in March 1976.

"Axe in hand the eighty-year-old Andries [sic] Marais stands in front of the house. I step back because the *oubaas* is clearly in a difficult mood.

"'I don't talk to newspaper people!' he says. His eyes are furious. 'You people are the reason The Hell is not the same anymore. Look at the nonsense you write about us!'

"It took a lot of soothing to calm *oom* Andries.

"He is one of Gamkaskloof's oldest residents. The bearded *oom*'s wife, *tant* Susanna, arrives and helps to calm him.

"'*Hartlam*,' (Darling) she says, "these people will surely not tell lies about us. How can you insult him like that?"

"*Oom* Andries's outrage is understandable. This tiny community in the mountains comprises 11 families and they have been portrayed in various publications as 'wild barbarians who run away from strangers'".

The journalist warns readers: "Stay away from Gamkaskloof if you do not have strong nerves. Particularly on a rainy day. Then you dare not attempt the road made by Rooi Kerneels [sic]. It twists and winds like a giant snake down the mountainside and rockfalls occur frequently.

"Should you come upon such a rockfall, the only choice is to reverse all the way back — and the driver who can do this, still has to be born."

Oom Andries thawed a bit and eventually chatted to the reporter.

"*Ja*! A visit to Gamkaskloof has already made several meek motorists swear that they will never ever again 'mount such a mad horse'.

"One day a *kêreltjie* (young man) stopped here with such a *bewerasie* (shakes) that we drove his car out for him.

"But," he adds, "The Hell is not what it used to be. There are telephones. And cars. And can you believe it, people actually get sick! *Voorjare* (Years ago) we knew no such things."

"*Tant* Susanna said she did not know much about The Hell. She had only lived there for 50 years.

"'The place is depopulating,' she said. 'Only the Mosterts, Swanepoels, Jouberts and a few others are left. Piet Mostert has turned forty and is about to marry. He's the youngest.'"

It is a fact that the exposure to outsiders was a powerful contribution to the exodus of residents. Irresponsible and unenlightened people ridiculed the Kloovers and their lifestyle. Children and young folk in particular were ashamed to admit their origins.

The few remaining families underwent a total personality change — particularly in the presence of strangers. This was propagated by various publications as "typical backwardness and retardation".

A journalist who wanted to interview Piet and Magriet Swanepoel was given a typical reception. An "after-the-road" reception!

He writes: "You feel when you approach them that they do not want you there.

"Magriet stood outside rearranging drying figs.

"She looked up quickly as soon as the greetings were over and said: 'My husband is in the vineyards,' and went inside.

"'*Ry maar aan!*' (ride on) said Piet when he chased them off his farm. 'Maybe the Mosterts will talk to you. Certainly not I!'

"At Hannes Mostert's home they were 'shown the road' equally hot-tempered.

"'You outsiders portray us as barbarians,' said his wife. 'Away with you! Leave us alone!'

"That this sort of behaviour was not at all typical of the Kloovers did not occur to many of the tourists. Or that they themselves were the reason that these, once-very-hospitable people acted like this.

"Koot, or maybe it was Karel, Cordier dealt with visitors in his own way."

Kloovers did, and do not, like the name The Hell. One day a backpacker passed him. He asked: "Do you perhaps know where Die Hel is?" Cordier told the fellow to carry on up Die Leer and beyond. "On the other side of the mountain you may find The Hell," he said.

"And," the tale ends, "he carried on."

Chris von Litzenbergh was a bachelor who moved in after the road.

After cross-examination by numerous visitors, he too became ill-tempered.

Chris, a descendant of the Cordiers, lived on 240 hectare and said "it is back-breaking to work alone."

"You really have to move when drying fruit and raisins. And," he boasted, "you name a vegetable, it grows here!"

For a Johnny-come-lately, Kloover Chris was abrupt to the point of rudeness when asked about his solitude.

"It's my own business!" he would snap.

Sometimes though, he was in a chatty mood.

"Pity the school is empty. In 1980 there were still four children who came *speel-speel* (playing) along Gamka to the school. Today, chickens live there," he explains.

Chris said he went to the "operational area" twice a year. He had a contract with the army to do border duty for a period of ten years and had to attend one camp annually.

"I do two!" he said. "The money is good!"

Without warning, he picks up his gun and shoots in the direction of the valley. Asked why, he says: "*Sommer*" (Because).

"My neighbour is Piet Swanepoel. If I go down and he's not at the gate, I do not see him at all. I don't walk to them. What's to talk about?"

Chris, in his insulated world became something of a philosopher. About the making of the Otto du Plessis road he says: "People are the problem. Fewer people, fewer problems!"

He taught himself to brew *karrie*. And tells of the *makietie* (party) that is held once a year. "Then the Kloof is right, my friend!" The town folks bring a *dingetjie* (something to drink). Then we start partying.

"I brew my *k'rie* for the occasion with young bees' bread (pollen) and the *moerbossie* in lukewarm water," he continues.

Chris does not farm with animals because of his regular departure to the border. But he explains the Mosterts and Swanepoels still keep goats. Although they have a devil of a problem with lynxes.

Chris has a tidy *fyntuin* (vegetable patch) and shows the pride of his garden, a pumpkin the size of his hat.

"I live off the land," he says.

When the spirit moves him, Chris takes a backpack and stays in the mountains for a week or longer.

"Once a month I go to town to buy things. On my scrambler. I had a *bakkie* (pick-up) but it's lying in a valley with all the other car skeletons. In town I had a few *krismisdoppe* (tots of brandy)!"

"The Swartberg looked like dragon's teeth. So I became drowsy. Ou Karel Cordier — who was bitten by the donkey — went with me in the *bakkie*. When the *bakkie* edged a bit too far and got stuck, I said: 'Oom Karel! *Oom* must remain just there!' Then we slowly climbed out and the *bakkie* went head over heels down the mountain.

"It's still there!"

How does he spend his leisure time?

"In quiet times I hunt! Have you ever tasted lynx? Softer than lamb," he says.

Lonely?

"Never! There's the radio. When the radio and I are on bad terms, it's me and my guitar," he explains.

"Here I work with candles. When the sun goes down I'm *in die vere* (in bed). I have a lot of books but I only look at the cover to know the story. I read them over and over again," he says.

Chris is regularly vexed by outsiders and their opinions.

"You people think we are all backward. Retarded. But we regularly have visitors from overseas. I accompany them to the beauty spots. I've even arranged hikes for them. But...," he concludes, "you people will never understand!"

Lenie Marais was another who remained in the Kloof for some time after the road. This even-tempered woman had an aversion to *buitemense* (outsiders). Many were students "who, under the guise of studying us came in to have orgies". As a monument of revenge she picked up their liquor bottles and built a hothouse. With the white, brown and green bottles she created interesting patterns when viewed from the inside. With the corks she made a frieze round the inside wall.

When her husband died she left.

The last family to leave Gamkaskloof was Piet and Magriet Swanepoel. One after the other preceded them. The Mosterts. The Cordiers, Koot, Karel and Stappies. The Jouberts acquired outside interests but retained their land and family homes. They came back. The Nels left.

When he moved in 1992, Piet Swanepoel said: "Why should one remain when everyone else has gone? I sold my farm to 'Flora and Fauna'. What do you do when you get old and sickly, and you're the only one left?"

Their home was the largest in the Kloof. Zannie and Anita manage The Hell from there.

The Swanepoels used their telephone as an extension of their activities, and fetched and carried for the few Kloovers whenever they went to town.

In 1981 the Kloof had a *nekslag* (setback) when a disastrous flood, which destroyed Laingsburg, also did inestimable damage in the Kloof. It so crippled the last few *vasbyters* (die-hards) that they left one after the other.

For five years, Piet and Magriet were the only remaining Kloovers. Until 1991.

Magriet did not look forward to life in town. Even with conveniences like electricity and television awaiting them. Such things did not excite her. She said: "We will long for our peace and quiet. The Kloof never angered us."

At the turn of the millennium the only ones left were David Jafta and Jan Claassen. At the end of the valley. They tend the Swiss goats and a few sheep.

No-one completely enjoyed moving out. Each had a personal reason. Piet Swanepoel put a heavy price on his privacy. This was counter-productive because it isolated him and Magriet. They were hospitable, but balked when visitors wanted Piet to talk about himself. This was unacceptable.

The Hell bled to death. Young people left never to return. Life outside was much easier and more exciting.

"Piet Swanepoel was a wise man," Kloovers say. "Long before he sold his farm he bought five hectares with a house in Prince Albert. He could afford to buy before he sold out in The Hell. Today Magriet benefits from this foresight."

Chapter thirteen
After the exodus

After the exodus from the Kloof, what was once fireside stories became *stoepstories* (tales). And as soon as someone heard that someone from The Hell was around, they were all ears.

Theo Olwage has indelible impressions about the term he taught there: "On my arrival I drove from Calitzdorp to Matjiesvlei and left my car at *oom* Broertjie Nel's farm. Broertjie asked one of his labourers to accompany me to the Kloof. Right up to the teacher's house. Before that, Broertjie explained where I could cross the Gamka and where I'd drown.

"The first few days I stayed with *tant* Martha and *oom* Freek Marais.

"It wasn't worth carrying in all my furniture for one term. This one loaned a bed, that one this and the other that. You have to cope with the bare minimum. I even made bamboo teaspoons.

"On the one side lived Hendrik Mostert and on the other side, Piet.

"Hendrik's yard was patioed with round pebbles, like a stable floor. When his daughter Marie married road-builder Koos van Zyl, I experienced my first Kloof wedding. And enjoyed it immensely! They had three brown musicians with concertina, mandoline and guitar. And we danced on the pebbled patio!

"Never as long as I live will I forget how we went out to buy groceries from Broertjie's farm. I offered my car.

"Beforehand they decided on the day. Everyone listens to the weather forecast for the Karoo on the radio because that is the Gamka River's catchment area.

"I offered my car. Four of us, a Marais, a Mostert and 63-year-old Snyman walked downstream. Something like 11 miles. Everyone carried a bag or packet of sugar.

"We walked to my car. From there to le Grange's shop.

"One after the other put his sack on the scale. Bought what was needed. So much flour and that much sugar and salt, and so on. When the bag showed a hundred pounds on the scale, each one picked it up and stopped buying.

"You must know a hundred pounds is *wragtag* (indeed) heavy! I took 50 lbs.

"We have to carry all this back!" he concludes.

Many Kloovers who left, worked at Gamka Dam after the road. It provided them with cash and a temporary income. Some went to the Railways in Beaufort West.

"We were not learned folk," they'll admit honestly, "and we couldn't do all sorts of work."

The change was not easy. And the longing for the Kloof omnipresent. In the injury time of their lives Koot and Karel Cordier lived in Prince Albert. In 1998 they were the last of the old school. At the end of 1998 Koot died.

But these two old rascals really stoked The Hell's fireside stories. And neither was an unwilling storyteller.

"Ja," Koot will sigh, "the Kloof is no longer the Kloof! Not since Otto du Plessis made the road. With that road came jealousies, hate and sins like that. Love and peace went out the other way. All of a sudden, our people had no more time for fellow human beings."

The next visitor or whoever had a willing ear, would hear *voortyd* (old-times) stories.

Says Koot to Karel: "You remember Spioenberg? When you creep into the hole, when you practically go down on your haunches you're in? *Dassiepis* (hyraceum)! Lots and lots of it? Now this fellow — not me — this fellow, tells me he was there. He lay flat on his stomach when he saw all the skeletons, skulls and bones and things. Heaps! He got the fright of his life when a porcupine moved among them. Right past him!"

Karel wants to talk about transport.

"It was a major thing to battle with pack donkeys up the Poort. One donkey pushes the other one and you truly *sukkel* (battle) with 35. Up the Poort. One wants to pass. Its sack falls into the water. You run to help him. Stop him. The others just carry on.

"You reload the donkey. PROPERLY!

"Now three donkeys rub against one another and the packs are skew. Some fall off. You fix this," Karel continues.

"Look!" interrupts Koot, clearly upset. "I don't want to hear about those things."

Whenever these two Kloovers chat, they still make a *wye draai* (digress) with their stories; typical of Kloof style.

Koot wants to tell about the sale of his property. He starts with Lewies Waarsêer who was so named "because he lied so much". He came in from Groenfontein.

"So your stepsister lets us know that her husband and Jan Hough of Prince Albert could no longer stay on the farm. Ferreira's children have all left. He stayed behind. Alone. Now he too wants to leave. We want to leave as well. Then 'the Englishman' came to *oorle' Pa* (late father). Underneath a black *olien* tree they *braaied*.

189

"Ferreira interprets for the Englishman. Tells him how many years ago the farm was paid off. It belonged to *oorle' Pa*. The overflow in the mountains belonged to Forestry.

"So we moved out. Now it's only Karel and I who are left," he sighs.

He sits quietly for a while.

"The old Griquas lived there in *voorjare* (long ago). With old Moses. Elandspad. That's where we farmed. Dried lots of fruit. Farmed well.

"You couldn't go to town every time. It is 54 miles there and back. You leave in the morning when the copper star comes out. You are 16 years old and you carry 60 lb out and 60 lb back. You undress before Die Poort. The river is filled with water. You put the bag on top of your head. Your clothes, everything, is on your head. Now you can go on to Calitzdorp."

Koot remains silent for a long time, clearly living through those days. Long, long ago.

Then he tells about his wedding and Kloof marriages.

"Those years we married in Prince Albert. Before you got home to celebrate your marriage, you had to turn back to have the baby christened." Had his wife Hester not smiled, you would have believed that Koot was serious.

"*Ja*, you needed *giftige voete* (nimble feet) in the Kloof. Like an ostrich. Because you have to go out at Teenek to the top where it disappears. When you go out to marry!

"That night you stopped over with people. Or in the hotel. You got married at nine o'clock and by ten you took the road back to the Kloof. Dark night and you were at Elandspas, if you crossed Weltevrede Mountain or Klippiesvlei.

"You danced all night. With those sore feet," he explains.

Again Koot gets lost in thought. Then he interrupts them with a totally different story.

"The policemen arrived. A police sergeant and a constable arrived. On horseback. So they rode. But beforehand they let *oorle' Pa* know they'll be there at a specific time.

"The sergeant drank a lot. Caused problems. He did so to get him going.

"They barked an order at my father: 'Give me your revolver!'

"'But I only shoot *tiers* in the mountains,' says my father.

"Now the sergeant asked for *witblits*.

"'Go and buy from Koot Hartman at Groenfontein. He has a licence. We don't do unlawful things.'

"By this time all our *blits* had been bottled or 'canned' and hidden. Just a small amount was left over.

"The sergeant drank.

"That night they slept outside on a spring mattress in front of the door. My brother-in-law had a guitar. He lay flat on his back. And played.

"The next day, when the copper star appeared, we had to feed their horses. They wanted to leave early.

"Grootboom and I saddled their horses. Then they stood at the front door.

"We left with the goats for the mountains.

"They asked for some *karrie*. As a fixer.

"When the sun rose, the sergeant mounted his horse, but his head banged on the road when he fell off.

"They then had to stay longer.

"Later *Ma* got tired of this nonsense and everyone helped to tie the sergeant to his horse so that he could remain seated to leave."

Koot remembers a story about the Anglo-Boer War: about "a certain Schoeman who came across on the footpath. He actually played the violin. His jaw was shot off during the war and *oorle' Ma* hid him. At Bopoort she cared for him. And fixed him.

"One day he explained where he had left his gun and dumdum bullets.

"He spoke to *oorle'* Kommandant Scheepers who waited at Dwyka River. (With Koot's stories you have to figure out where he is heading, as an interruption derails the story completely.)

"With him was a group of Basters. They saw a strange *spoor* (footprint). It must have passed *voor-dag* (before day-break). They sighted him within gun range and shot him *middelpaadjie* (grazing his head) through his hat.

"There he lay," continues Koot with the story which other Kloovers tell about a honey-thief. "He thought he was dead. He remained lying. They undressed him, took all his bullets and his Lee Metford.

"His sleeping place was in a cave.

"Next morning they looked for him and he was gone."

Karel takes over.

"The Mosterts still have their land. After all these years.

"Father's bosom friend Piet van Wyk always said: 'We too will see that our children get the land just like we got it.' And now? Two-thirds of the Kloof belonged to my father before he sold it."

Should you think this is the end of the Cordier *stoepstories* (folklore) and get ready to leave, you find out this was the prologue.

Koot shocks you back onto your seat with the blunt statement: "The Kloof was full of murderers!"

Typical Cordier style — dead pan — he tells how they dealt with Swartjanfrans.

"He had a child with Swartjan's *klimmeid* (maid). So *die ou* (the fellow) took his gun and shot him.

"Then one day he sat on his haunches amongst the pumpkins. A Baster comes along the footpath, carrying a yellow ewe. She had not yet lambed. He slits her throat.

"A *karee* tree nearby had toppled over and he picked up a thick branch and killed him with it! He dragged him to the river. There he threw him in a hole and covered it up with stones. He named it *Jan-se-gat* (Jan's hole)."

Hester sits quietly smiling all the time. Saying nothing. If people want to believe all Koot's tales it is their own affair. Kloovers are used to telling stories. And making up riddles.

Koot's chatting dries up again.

"Ja! Today I wish I was gone! Just gone! There's nothing left in life."

Hester ignores this and says that when they moved out, Koot brought a milch goat but she did not take to town life.

"Ja!" sighs Koos again, "now I have nothing. Just this house. And Hester can have it.

"How old am I now, *vrou* (wife)? I think about sixty-four? It's a wonder I'm still here after all the hardship."

When one enters the sitting-room, Koos does not sit on a chair but on his haunches.

"It's because of the goat minding in the mountains. In the veld you sit like that and you get used to it," explains Hester.

Both Koot and Hester were born in Gamkaskloof. Koot said he never really bothered with outside girls. "Didn't know how," he admits.

Hester says it's partially true but he must not admit it to outside people.

"Koot has regarded himself *grootmeneer* (big shot) ever since his youth," she says. "All the *karrie*! Those young bees in the *karrie* made him very amorous.

"He was twenty-one when we were married," she says.

"*Ja!*" says Koot, "and we have three-and-a-half dozen children!"

Hester still laughs at Koot's joke, and adds: "Yes! Seven girls and two boys!"

"The elder ones did not have an easy time. They were born before the road and had to walk across Swartberg Mountain to school and back.

"Terrible days!" says Koot.

"Fortunately, our house was large enough. Four rooms. When the five younger children were born, the elder four were out. Married. Out. I was sorry about that. We Kloovers always stood united."

Then he almost smiles: "Our children are good people.

"Even when the Kloof still had only a hundred people living there it was a pleasant place. Particularly the dancing. *Karrie* and all. I was a *voordanser* (lead dancer) and *die meisiegoed* (girls) couldn't leave me alone," he brags. Hester agrees.

"*Vrou!* What was our farm called?" asks Koot.

"Baviaanskloof!" Hester replies.

"*Ja!*" says Koot. "Baviaanskloof!"

All of it sold. Quite a piece of land. "And did we eat well! *Boerbok* (goat)! Once you've tasted *boerbok* you'll never eat lamb or mutton again."

A long silence falls on the group again.

Koot breaks it.

"And now I'm 'under the doctors'. They can do nothing about my blood pressure. And today I feel terrible. I wish I were gone!" he laments.

"And that," says Hester, "I've heard for many years."

Now that Koot is actually gone, one wishes him a peaceful and blessed rest. Although he was burried in Prince Albert and not in The Hell.

194

Epilogue

When entering The Hell there is often a distinct Bodorp (uptown) and Onderdorp (downtown) feeling, even though you know it is all one place. You feel the Bodorp was on the other side of the river and the Onderdorp this side.

In the *voorjare* (early times) there was a unique "attitude". Bodorpers invited visitors into the *voorhuis*. Onderdorpers say people seldom came into their *voorhuis*. Their gathering place was the kitchen. The *voorhuis* was for strangers and the *dominee*.

Bodorp seems to have more farmlands because of abundant water. This is where Piet Mostert many moons ago earned pound for pound for his excellent onion seed. Under the age-old pepper tree in Bodorp the threshing machine, which cleaned the seed, can still be seen.

A stranger notices that the fields in the Onderdorp are smaller with less water and longer irrigation furrows leading to the crops.

At the end of the millennium Zannie and Anita van der Walt are the top officials. They have lived there for almost a decade. Both are hospitable and good conversationalists. They have not once regretted their decision to live in the Kloof.

The Hell hosts many guests. In 1997, for instance, from January to December they recorded 2 700 visitors. It has since grown to 9 000 a year. This excludes those at "The Doctors". They too found many people ill-prepared for a visit, with no idea what to expect.

"Where is The Hell?" one will ask. Another wants to know: "How do you get out on the other side?" Or "What's to see?" or "to do?".

"You show them the walking trails, the houses, the mountains, the ravines and they say: 'Oh that! Thanks. Not for me!'

Anita says many people drive in for a visit and a chat. About the Kloof's history. Tradition. Habits. They want to know everything. Everything. They never get enough of Kloof stories.

"Lots of foreigners," she says.

Anita tells tourists the best way to get to know Gamkaskloof is with *dapper en stapper* (hiking). "That's how you see the place like the Kloovers knew it. The slopes invite, almost dare you to climb them," she says.

The fields, orchards and vineyards are skeletons, but the memories and the signs are there. Small streams and rivulets are constantly in your way. Trees aplenty. And birds. And if you spot only one eagle, your tour is perfect.

Zannie and Anita often pay Kloovers and their relatives a visit when they go out to Prince Albert, Oudtshoorn or Calitzdorp. All of them enjoy the contact and a good chat.

Not only do the Van der Walts enjoy the company, but it's often conversation pieces for the record. And with which to regale visitors!

"I always warn them," says Zannie, "that like all Kloof stories, mine are 10 per cent truth and 90 per cent lies." And he copies Koot Cordier's straight-faced pose. For the few remaining "permanent" residents: Jan Claasen and his wife, the Jouberts, Zannie and Anita, Bennie, Annetjie and their son Pieta, labourers are not readily available but they cope. At the end of the millennium, they have replanted hanepoot vineyards and pruned the trees, Annetjie makes fig jam and dried figs as her ancestors did and runs her Kloof property for the joy of everyone.

The Department of Nature Conservation is sometimes criticised for the slow pace of restoration, as houses seem to be decaying. In some cases, pine wood was used as a temporary measure in restoration — a type of wood not used in the Kloof.

But there are many plus points. Lenie Marais's home was restored.

In 1992 the Middelplaas teacher's home was restored and turned into a guest house.

Specialists in several disciplines are doing valuable studies in the Kloof, and of the Kloof.

Although the need and eagerness to restore the place is recognised, a lack of funding handicaps speedy restoration.

Houses older than 50 years are historic monuments. Zannie would like to see the whole of Gamkaskloof declared a Nature Reserve and conserved as such. He dreams that a trust might be founded to finance future development.

The possibilities for education and research are endless.

And Zannie dreams of bringing in lay people to help with the running of the farms.

Anita shares these sentiments: "It will be a tragedy if The Hell should lose its holistic nature."

This couple's enthusiasm and love spills over to visitors.

"There is so much to see and experience! Just think of the Bushman paintings! There's even a yellow elephant. And the winding roads to the cottages, everyone worth a visit," she explains enthusiastically.

Talking to an informed visitor like Theo Olwage you learn the true spirit in which to visit The Hell.

"A visit is worthwhile when you enter through one of the historical routes. We slept above Die Leer the first night and truly experienced how cold The Hell really is."

Ever think Hell does not freeze over? It does! And it did!

"At half past nine our sleeping bags were white when frost turned to ice," Theo remembers.

"Die Leer was terrible! Steep! That anything could be transported up or down even on pack donkeys is mind-boggling.

"One realises why horses balked at going up or down.

"At the foot of the mountain where Die Leer stops, there's a mountain stream. The emerald-green grass is soft. There are a few trees. When you lie down there to rest your exhausted, aching body, the biblical Psalm 23 comes to mind: green pastures, peace and water. You know that the poet David must have been in such a place when he wrote it.

"Five kilometres along you encounter the friendliness and hospitality of Kloof people.

"Piet Mostert's juicy, flavoursome *naartjies* are incomparable.

"Six kilo's further and we're on the banks of the Gamka River. You bathe in the ice-cold water. Refreshing! Your body is no longer tired. Or aching. A small fire, a chop on the spit, a sleeping bag, the singing of the *klipslanertjies* (birds) in the background and what more do you want?

"The second day you walk *kuier-kuier* (leisurely) and *kyk-kyk* (observant) up to where Lewies Waarsêer's house is.

"Talk about chatting. A day is much too short.

"Tonight you get into your sleeping bag on the banks of the Gamka and you think: 'What have I learnt today?' You know you have truly found out what it is to be *'n mens* (human being). Spiritually rejuvenated. You realise your own insignificance when the gigantic mountains tower above you and the sound of falling water seems forever. You look up from the depths below to the slice of blue heaven above. You realise you are breathing freely. Time is not a factor any more. It was worth it!

"Only when you return and come up against the wall of the Gamka Dam, which spans a previous exit route, do you realise that you're again confronted with the work of human hands."

A foreign visitor once wrote: "The most spectacular natural scenes in Southern Africa is to be seen in the Swartberg Mountains.

"From the Cango caves side you zig-zag for 10 km up an awesome slope with the forbidding weirs on the mountain range, along the dirt road of (Thomas) Bain.

"From the Prince Albert side it seems you're going to crash into vertical mountain sides at every twist and turn which crawls up a narrow kloof.

"You are surrounded by chalk rock formations like giant pink castles.

"Out of this 'chaos' of mountainsides, you climb upwards along hairpin twists on slopes of which the formations are tortuous, in waves and loops made by the powers of creation in aeons past."

This truly is what a visit to Gamkaskloof can do to a person who visits it with the correct attidue.

You get a glimpse, a notion, of a link with not only the *voorjare* (earliest times) or *voortye*, not only with natural forces, but with powers of forgotten and bygone eras.

Sources

Interviews.

Gemeente onder die Swartberg — NG Kerk Prins Albert: PJ en M Botes.

An Approximate history of Gamkaskloof — PM Ferreira (pamphlet).

Oudtshoorn Courant — many issues.

Toegewaaide Voetspore in 'n Bergvallei — Gerbrechta Burger (Unpublished).

CP Nel Museum — Oudtshoorn.

Francie Pienaar Museum — Prince Albert.

Die Burger — several articles.

Country Life — (July/Aug 1998).

Commando — Deneys Reitz.

People of the Valley — Life in an Isolated Afrikaner Community — BM du Toit, University of Florida.

Kalahari Bushmen — Alan Barnard.

The Bushmen — Alf Wannenburg.

Gamkaskloof Verlore Vallei — Koos van Zyl (unpublished).

Die Kultuurhistorikus — Nov. 1997. University of Stellenbosch.

Rapport Ateljee — April 1984.

Hell (Gamkaskloof): Dr Pieter Christoffel Luttig. (Unpublished).

SA Panorama — several issues.

The Little Karoo — José Burman.

Historica — April 1987. (Holland).

Weekend Argus — March 1988.

Personality — Feb. 1967.

Gamkaskloof — "Die Hel": J Vorster (University of Cape Town 1992. Hist/Arch project.)

Landstem — Oktober 1958.

Report on Gamkaspoort Government Waterworks — PH Nel. Department of Agriculture and Forestry.

Die Brandwag — 14 February 1935.

Library — Ladismith.

Groot Woordeboek Afr/Eng: Kritzinger, Schoonees & Cronje.

Restorica: 1987.